The Dog

WITH THE

Old Soul

**TRUE STORIES OF THE LOVE,
HOPE AND JOY THAT ANIMALS
BRING TO OUR LIVES**

Jennifer Basye Sander

HARLEQUIN® NON-FICTION

The Dog with the Old Soul
ISBN: 978 0 263 90534 2
© 2012 by Jennifer Basye Sander

Published in Great Britain 2013
Harlequin, an imprint of Harlequin (UK) Limited,
Eton House, 18-24 Paradise Road,
Richmond, Surrey, TW9 1SR

Printed and bound by
CPI Group (UK) Ltd, Croydon, CR0 4YY

CONTENTS

Contents

Contents

INTRODUCTION

"An animal anthology? Really? You?" new friends may ask upon hearing about this book project, looking around my well-ordered house, devoid of cat hair or a wet-dog smell. What gives? There are no bags of pet food in my garage. My newspaper is recycled promptly, never placed at the bottom of a birdcage. Older friends nod in understanding, though, since they knew the Airedale that lives on forever in my heart.

Animals take up residence in our hearts, sometimes consuming all available space and leaving no room for another dog, cat, horse or bird to be added to the mix. I love dogs, but I haven't had one myself in years. Just like some people have only one perfect love in their lives and, once it is over, don't feel the need to replace it, my dog Big Guy spoiled me as an owner. I delight in having others' pets around me, though, and I love to watch the affection and interaction between animals and people.

We are devoted to our animals, and they can be just as devoted to us. A recent news item touched everyone who stumbled upon it—the story of a man in China who passed away, leaving only a yellow dog behind. The dog refused to leave his grave, lying atop it day after day. Villagers brought the dog food and water, and one resident told reporters that the sight of the grieving dog "made my heart smile and cry."

The stories in *The Dog with the Old Soul* will also make your heart both smile and cry. There are stories of joy—the thrill of a new puppy, the excitement of a young girl's first horse show ribbon, the silliness of a room filled with cats. But life isn't always joyful, and there are stories of the comforting role that animals can play in our emotional lives. There are times in life when reaching down to pet a familiar fuzzy head can help ground us in a way nothing else can.

It is my hope that these stories touch you deeply, and that more than once while reading, you reach out and pull your pets in closer to you on the couch. Enjoy!

Jennifer Basye Sander

The Dog with the Old Soul

Finley Taylor

Sometimes people—or in my case, a dog—come into your life at just the right time.

Even before we were married, my husband and I talked about the dogs we would get someday. I wanted a Scottish terrier; he wanted a basset hound. Both of us liked both dogs, and neither of us minded which one we got first. We eventually decided that since bassets were known for being calm, low maintenance and child friendly—and since we were planning on having children soon—we'd get a basset first. Only problem was, for the first year and a half of our marriage we lived in a tiny apartment in Midtown.

When we moved to a larger home in 2009, it was time to start thinking about getting a dog. Well, actually, it was time to start thinking about having those children. Getting a dog was something we might push off till after the first baby was born, we thought. But the months went by and the pregnancy tests kept turning up negative.

The thought of including a different type of being, one with four legs, as part of our family never was far from our thoughts. As much as we talked about baby names and family vacations and how we would *not* give our eight-year-old a cell phone, we also talked about hiking trips and strolls along the river and what we'd name our dog.

Three days after my twenty-seventh birthday, my husband sent me a seemingly innocuous photo from a local shelter's website of a perky-looking tricolored basset hound with intelligent, old-soul eyes. Her name was Chloe.

I work from home, so the squeal I let out fell on an otherwise silent house—a silence that over the months had developed a pitch of frustration, sadness and worry that became more palpable with each Facebook pregnancy announcement I saw. I called my husband and asked if he was game to go look at the pup with the world-heavy expression.

That night we stood outside the kennel of a loudly barking Chloe, who seemed to be conveying her frustration at being cooped up for so long, and at life for being a little rough on her as of late.

I didn't blame her. A kind but frazzled shelter

employee told us this was the second time Chloe had been brought to the shelter.

Chloe let out a characteristic basset bark that rumbled deep in my bones, rattling loose feelings of compassion and a desire to care for another living being—feelings I'd lately been walling off in an act of self-preservation. My husband and I looked at each other. "Let's go home and sleep on it," I said.

When we told the front-desk clerk that we needed a night to ponder adopting Chloe, she said, "You know, a family adopted her and brought her back ten days later because she had a cut on her leg. A cut." The disdain in her voice stung my ears. It appeared this pup would not be given away again without the blessing of some very strong gatekeepers.

The next night we were back at the shelter, ready to adopt Chloe. My jangled thoughts and emotions zipped about my brain as if I were a kid in a bounce house. *Are we ready for this? Can we be good enough guardians for her? Our lives are about to change.*

"She's a very vocal dog," said a frazzled employee, this one with a platinum blond ponytail, while opening the kennel.

Chloe *aoooff*ed nonstop out of impatience.

A cage that had not been cleaned out recently and a pen in which a matted microfleece blanket lay on the cold concrete were evidence of what the staff had already told us: the new shelter was struggling to survive, even as it tried to house a growing number of animals.

We were allowed to let this feverish canine out and to walk her, and she immediately put her nose to the ground with the loving familiarity of a mother tracing a finger over her child's face. Within minutes, our hearts were completely won over by a panting, slobbering, smelly tank of infectiously lovable dog.

"We'd like to adopt Chloe," we announced at the front desk.

"Adoptions ended a half hour ago," said the front desk person, who was a different woman than the night before. Her name tag read "Staci."

Crushed, we went home, nonetheless determined to be there right when the shelter opened the next day.

We arrived ten minutes before the shelter opened, and a coldness that didn't come from the damp December air enveloped me when I saw about a half dozen other people in front of us in line.

"Are they all here to adopt?" I whispered to my husband. "You don't think someone here wants to adopt Chloe, do you?"

My husband gave me a look. "Well, we'd better hightail it to the front desk as soon as possible," he said.

When the front doors opened, we were the first to the desk. Staci, the woman who had turned us down the night before, was working again today. She smiled, pushing a lock of cocoa-brown hair out of her face. "You're here to adopt the basset hound."

We nodded like fools.

"I'll go get her." She rose to leave the desk, then turned to face us. "You know, she's very vocal."

We made assuring noises and stepped back when she sent a volunteer to get Chloe. A mother and two teenage girls came up to the desk. The mother said to an employee behind the desk—the one with the platinum blond ponytail who had allowed us to open Chloe's pen the night before—"We're here to adopt Chloe, the basset hound."

Our eyes went wide. *Wait, not* our *basset.*

"We were here last night," the mother explained, "and started to fill out paperwork, but they said we couldn't adopt her, because it was too late."

The blond employee, who had not heard our conversation a moment ago with Staci at the front desk, said, "Okay, I'll go get her."

My husband went up to Staci, who had just sent the volunteer to retrieve Chloe. "I don't want to cause a scene, but we just heard someone say they wanted to adopt the basset that you're getting for us."

Staci looked at us. "Oh." She got the attention of the blond employee, who came back to the desk and listened as Staci told our story.

"Yeah, I remember you," said the blond woman. "But this family did start the paperwork." They looked at each other, and then the blond woman hurried to the back, where the volunteer was supposedly getting "our" dog.

How could this happen?

We had tried twice to take Chloe home, we knew we were ready for her, and now our little addition might be ripped away from us before we even had a chance to have her. We looked at the other family discreetly. They looked nice enough, with their perfect white smiles and their matching sweatshirts with their private high school's name emblazoned on them. But she was supposed to be *our* dog.

Finally, the blond woman came back, holding the leash to Chloe, who was elated to be outside her kennel. We and the other family stood there awkwardly. The blond woman walked up to me and held out the leash. "Here you go," she said.

I looked at the leash in my hand. And smiled at it.

Twenty minutes later, after filling out enough paperwork to apply for a home loan, we walked out of the shelter the proud new guardians of a vocal, four-year-old basset hound, our hearts still stinging a bit at the image in our minds of the disappointed teenagers as they dejectedly walked past us to go home empty-handed. We never found out why the shelter chose us over the other family.

On the way to the car, we called our newest family member by the name we had chosen the night before, Bridgette— a name we felt encapsulated her unique, sweet yet spunky nature. We later found out that the name means "the exalted one" and "one who is strong and protective."

"Do you think she's happy to be out of there?" my husband asked, trying to get a look at her through the rearview window as he drove. I looked at the backseat, where Bridgette, with her long, thick body, flung herself onto her side like a breaching whale and breathed a contented sigh.

Four months later I was diagnosed with infertility, and we discovered that the only way we could have a biological family of our own was by in vitro fertilization. As I underwent testing and surgery, Bridgette was steadfast. And as I await a risky and uncertain treatment, she remains at my feet, showing a constancy that throws into sharp relief the actions of those in her previous life, those who had been entrusted with her care—a constancy that challenges me to return what she has given me. I stand at a threshold, facing an uncertain future of my own, and her old-soul eyes serve as a daily reminder of grace as I am brought through the doors of a temporary holding place that I hope will eventually lead me home.

Simon Says

Katherine Traci

November. Dark. Cold. I was driving home from a late-night writing workshop, a brutal night of fellow writers casually critiquing what was my own heart typed out neatly on the page. The exact same heart that had been trampled on by a liar three weeks prior. We'd gone to Venice to fall more deeply in love, cement it all in ancient stone. But no. Instead the medieval city was the scene of a modern breakup.

"Good plan, Kate," I scoffed to myself in my car, gripping the wheel and picturing what I should have done instead—pushed him into the dirty Grand Canal. I hadn't pushed him in. I'd gotten on the plane home like a good girl and flown back to an empty house, an empty heart. Tonight I'd hoped that writing it down and sharing it, letting others know how I felt, would help me heal. And maybe it would in the long run; but right then, alone, surrounded by strangers, empty and at a loss, I sat waiting to turn left onto the dark on-ramp, headed home. My head turned to follow a tiny cat that streaked across the road as it crossed my line of vision.

Feral, I thought as it headed toward the freeway. Odd behavior for any smart feral that lived in the area. I watched as what I now saw was a kitten run up the embankment toward a busy freeway overpass. It was almost 10:00 p.m. and the street was empty. I was tired . . . I was hungry . . . I was sad . . . I wanted to be home. The light changed. I stayed where I was.

Hmm, well timed on behalf of the cat, I thought. I had left class at the right second, had driven the right speed, had paused just long enough to turn at the exact moment that the little cat decided to sprint across six full lanes of the street in front of my truck.

Sighing, I felt the full weight of my own empty life hit me. If I couldn't push a man in a canal, at least I could rescue a kitty on the side of the road. I pulled over as far as possible onto the left shoulder and hit my hazards. There he was, hunkered down in the greenery far above me. I rolled down my window. I watched the kitten. The kitten watched me. I got out of the car.

I looked up the steep embankment at him. *Ice plant. Damn.* It was cold. I am a 911 dispatch operator. For me, hazards lurk everywhere, even in the safest of homes. A slippery shower, a frayed electrical cord. So many of the calls we take are the result of foolhardy behavior. This would fall easily into that category.

I have nothing to put a cat in. I don't even have a blanket. I have no idea what I am doing, I thought as I looked around. *And I'm mostly a dog girl. I'll go out of my way to rescue dogs. But a cat?* I shivered and tried to focus on a workable plan.

I decided to try and approach him. If he ran up toward the top of the embankment, I'd have to back off. I didn't want to be responsible for a cat on a busy freeway. I started up the steep embankment and the kitten didn't move. He blinked at me. He sat in the ice plant near the freeway on-ramp and slowly blinked his big teary eyes, open, shut, open. The light shone down from the streetlamp and his eyes glowed. Open. Shut.

I clutched at the fence along the embankment with one hand and made my way up the slippery ice plant. It was a good slope. My clumsiness well known, I tried to keep out of my head the images of me tumbling back down to the asphalt below.

I could hear the morning news in my head: "An unidentified woman tried to climb ice plant in an attempt to access the freeway for unknown reasons. She was unkempt and messy, and all evidence suggests she suffers from broken heart syndrome. The authorities have hesitated to confirm or deny this, and it is unknown at this time if this syndrome is related to last night's incident. She is in critical but stable condition today at the medical center, after falling twenty feet. Doctors say she fell sometime late last night and was not discovered until morning."

I was one foot away. I could touch him if I reached out. Should I take off my hoodie to grab him and wrap him up?

Nooo, I thought as I zipped the hoodie up further. *It's too cold.*

I pulled the hoodie's wrist cuffs down over my hands, minimal protection against claws at best, and stretched out toward him. I aimed for the back of his neck.

Cat scratch fever, cat scratch fever…cat scratch fever! My dad's voice reverberated in my head. Whether it was a warning or the lyrics to a song, I couldn't quite remember.

I reached out once…twice…three times. Each time the kitty turned his head around to look at my hand but didn't move.

Oh. I'm going to pick him up and he will be a bloody mess, badly injured, I thought, feeling sick to my stomach in addition to feeling cold. I could see only his tiny head. And those big blinking eyes.

Really, this was too absurd. Remember, I see potential danger everywhere. Yet there I was on a dark, cold night, perched on a slope of ice plant near a freeway overpass in the middle of a part of town you really shouldn't slow down in, let alone pull over and stop in. I was alone, trying to rescue a damn kitten.

I needed to get this over with. "Now or never. Just do it, Kate!" And with that rallying cry I grabbed him and pulled him to my chest. His claws held on to me and I felt his body vibrate with his purrs. I looked down the embankment. Now I had to make my way back down. This time with no hands to hold on to the fence, as both were clasping this mess of a cat. Tense, I carefully picked my way with each step down the slippery ice plant on the steep embankment, arriving at the bottom without incident.

In what felt like a one-take action sequence, I threw the car door open, tossed the kitten in, grabbed my keys, started the car, rolled up the window—before the rescued cat escaped! I turned to look at him. He was perched expectantly on my center console, waiting and watching my hurried antics. He was bones. Skin and bones…and purrs.

Next morning at the vet's office, they insisted on a name. I stood in front of the receptionist, shaking my head.

"I'm not going to name him. I don't want to name him."

The receptionist raised her eyebrows and cocked

her head, her fingers hovering over the keys of her computer.

"Please don't make me name him. I can't keep him. I have a very small house."

She waited. This same scene must have happened a lot here. I wondered if it always turned out the same way. "Okay, we'll just type in k-i-t-t-y."

"No, don't write 'Kitty' on the chart. I don't want to call him Kitty." Something told me his name was Simon.

Simon spent the next two weeks sequestered in my bathroom, my only bathroom. I gingerly opened the door whenever I needed access, pushing my foot in ahead of me to keep Simon from rushing the door, nudging him out of the way if he made an attempt to escape. I needed to keep him away from my other pets, the vet said, until the lab results came in and they gave him a clean bill of health.

So until that approval came through, I had a four-pound, voraciously hungry, frustratingly messy roommate. A *loud* roommate who lived exclusively in my bathroom. His tortured cries reverberated off the tile when he heard me stir in any part of the house. In an effort to calm him, I'd visit for long periods of time, just sitting on the edge of the tub. Talking seemed to quiet him down, so I talked. The look in his eyes made me feel that he could answer back.

"My mom died, Simon," I whispered.

"When?" he would purr, rubbing his cheek against mine.

"Two years ago, but it still hurts."

"I know," he would squeak, "but then somebody comes along and helps." He reached out a paw to tap my nose.

Simon talks to everything and everyone. He has a sweet *meep,* high pitched and soft, when looking up at me; a *brrrrr* chirp when he asks my older, "can hardly be bothered" cat relentlessly for playtime; and he gives a *merrwrrrow* to the dog whenever their eyes lock. All very different sounds, very specific and very Simon.

Simon believes he has an imaginary friend. When he plays with crumpled-up paper, he growls and chirps and looks around and plays…with somebody. Not me. Not my other cat. Not my dog. He is alone. It is the craziest thing to watch. The tiny noises he makes scare the bejesus out of my big, scary dog.

Since I found him on the way home from a writing class, perhaps he is a writer, too. He has a special fondness for laptop keyboards. The first time it was the letter *x*. I found him batting something small and black—the key off the keyboard—around the floor, like a hockey player practicing with a puck. The next time it was the *t*. He leaps up and pounces on the unattended keyboard. No letter is safe as he picks whichever one he pleases to pry off and play with. The third time it was *b* and *e,* double the fun. They recognize me now at the computer repair shop.

The little ice-plant kitty was the most loving creature I had ever met. I thought I'd left my capacity for love squashed flat on the cobblestones in Italy, but Simon taught me my heart was still there, strong and healthy, after all.

Sometimes I look at Simon and think back to that night on the side of the freeway. I think I saved Simon, but maybe he saved me.

Where the Need Is Greatest

Tish Davidson

I have been a volunteer puppy raiser with Guide Dogs for the Blind for ten years. Donna Hahn has been raising guide dogs for at least twice that long. She has shared tips on socializing puppies, has helped me with difficult dogs and has encouraged me when my dogs failed to make the grade as guides. We have traded puppy-sitting chores and dog stories. Donna has loved every guide dog puppy she has ever raised. But one dog was special. This is Donna's story.

Donna could hardly control her tears as she mounted the platform at the outdoor graduation ceremony. A light breeze ruffled the flag. The audience waited, polite and attentive. The graduates sat, alert and poised. The flag had been saluted; the speeches made;

the staff and students congratulated. Now it was time to take the final step and send the graduates out into the world to fulfill their mission.

Donna stopped beside one of the graduates and rested a hand on his shoulder. "Raising a puppy is an act of love and faith," she began. "When a puppy comes into your home, he comes into your heart. He is a part of your family. You give him all the time, care and love you can. Then, almost before you know it, that curious, wriggling, uncoordinated puppy has changed into an obedient, mature dog, ready to return to Guide Dogs for the Blind and take the next step in becoming a working guide.

"I'm thrilled and happy that Llama—" she indicated the golden retriever next to her "—has become a working guide. But I'm sad, too, because it is always hard to say goodbye to someone you love." She picked up Llama's leash and handed it to Gil, Llama's new partner. "Goodbye, Llama. You are a special dog."

The crowd murmured in appreciation, and some in the audience sniffled audibly and reached for their tissues. Then the graduation was over. Soon Llama and Gil were on their way to Vancouver, Canada, and Donna was on her way home to Newark, California, knowing there was a good chance she would never see Llama again.

Llama was the third puppy the Hahn family—

Donna, John, and their daughters, Wendy and Laurel— had raised for Guide Dogs for the Blind, but he was the first to complete the program and become a working guide. He had come into their life fifteen months earlier, a red-tinged golden retriever with white hairs on his face and muzzle that gave him a washed-out, unfinished look. "An ugly dog," Donna had said at the time. But soon his looks didn't matter.

At first, Llama was as helpless as any new baby. "Neee, neee, neee," he cried when he was left alone. He woke Donna in the night and left yellow abstract designs on the carpet when she didn't get him out the door fast enough. Donna patiently cleaned up the accidents. Soon Llama learned "Do your business," one of the early commands that every guide dog puppy learns, and the accidents rapidly decreased.

Like all guide pups, Llama was trained with love and kind words, rather than with food treats. Soon he would follow Donna through the house on his short puppy legs, collapsing at her feet when she said, "Sit," happy to be rewarded with a pat and a "Good dog."

Llama seemed to double in size overnight. By the time he was five months old, he was accompanying Donna everywhere. It wasn't always easy. Llama had to learn to overcome his natural inclination to sniff the ground and greet every dog he met on the street. At the supermarket he learned not to chase the wheels on the grocery cart. At Macy's he learned to wait while Donna tried on clothes. With a group of other puppies in training, Llama and Donna rode the ferry across San Francisco Bay and toured the noisy city.

In May Donna was summoned for jury duty in superior court in Oakland. Of course, she took Llama. Privately, she hoped that his presence would be enough to get her automatically excused, but the plan backfired. For a week, Llama lay patiently at Donna's feet in the jury box while Donna attended the trial.

All too soon, a year was up, and the puppy that had wagged its way into Donna's heart was a full-grown dog, ready to return to the Guide Dogs campus in San Rafael and start professional training. There was only a fifty-fifty chance he would complete the program. Working guides must be physically and temperamentally perfect before they are entrusted with the life of a blind person. Donna had given Llama all the love and training she could; now his future was out of her hands.

Llama passed his physical and sailed through the training program. When it came time to be matched with a human partner, the young golden retriever was paired with Gil, a curator at an aquarium in Canada. Matching dog and human is a serious and complicated ballet in which the dog's strengths, weaknesses and personality are balanced against the human's personality and lifestyle. When done well, an unbreakable bond of love and trust develops between human and dog.

Gil and Llama were a perfect match, and their bond grew strong and true. Gil had never had a guide dog before. Once home, he found that Llama gave him a new sense of confidence, independence and mobility. Every day they walked together along the seawall to Gil's work at the aquarium. In time, everyone grew to know Llama, and Llama grew to know all the sights and sounds of Gil's workplace. For ten years, Llama was at Gil's side every day—at home, at work, on vacation, and on trains, planes and buses.

Meanwhile, at the Hahns', Wendy and Laurel grew up and moved away from home. John and Donna continued to raise pups. Their fourth dog became a family pet. The fifth became a working guide in Massachusetts, and the sixth a service dog for a physically handicapped teen.

While they were raising their seventh pup, Donna's husband, John, a fit and active air force veteran, began having stomach problems. An endoscopy revealed the bad news. John had advanced gastric cancer. Thus began a long series of treatments and operations to try to catch the cancer, which always seemed one step ahead of the surgeon's knife. It was a grim, sad, stress-filled time. Soon John could no longer take any nourishment by mouth. With John's strength waning daily, the family came to accept that he had only a few months to live.

In October, with John desperately ill, a call came from the Guide Dogs placement advisor. "Donna, we just got a call that Llama is being retired. He's been working for ten years, and all that stair-climbing and leading tours at the aquarium have caught up with him. He has pretty bad arthritis. Gil is coming down to train with a new dog. I know John is terribly sick, and the last thing you might want to do right now is take care of an old dog, but Gil specifically requested that we ask you if you could give Llama a retirement home. He can't keep Llama himself, but he wants him to be with someone who will love him."

"Of course we'll take him," said Donna, never hesitating.

Several days later Donna drove up to the Guide Dogs campus to pick up Llama. She paced back and forth across the receiving area as she waited for a kennel helper to bring Llama to her.

"Do you think he'll recognize me after ten years?" she anxiously asked an assistant in a white lab coat.

When Llama arrived, moving stiffly in the damp morning air, it was not the joyous reunion she had imagined. Llama seemed pleased to see her, but in a reserved, distant way. An hour and a half later, Llama was back at the house where he had spent the first year of his life.

Donna pushed open the front door. "John, we're home." Llama didn't hesitate for a second. He walked in, turned and headed straight into John's bedroom, as if he had been going there every day of his life. From that moment on, he rarely left John's bedside. Although he was too old to guide, Llama had found a place where he was needed.

Llama was a careful and gentle companion for John. When John got out of bed, pushing the pole that held his intravenous feeding bottles, Llama was beside him, ready to protect him, but careful never to get in his way or get tangled in the medical apparatus.

"I don't know how that dog always seems to know exactly what you need, but he surely does," said Donna more than once.

"He was sent to take care of me," John replied.

By the end of the month, John's condition had worsened. The hospice nurse administered morphine. Donna was afraid the drug would make John disoriented and that he would try to get out of bed and would fall over Llama, so she ordered the dog to leave the room.

"Llama, out."

Llama, who had never disobeyed a command, didn't budge.

"Llama, out."

Llama didn't move a muscle and remained planted by John's bed.

The next morning, however, Llama began to pace frantically back and forth through the house.

"What's wrong with him, Mom?" asked Wendy, who had come home to help her mother.

"I don't know. Maybe he's sick."

The pacing continued all day and into the evening.

At 9:30 that night, John passed away. Llama stopped pacing and lay quietly by the door.

"He must have known the end was near," said Wendy.

Llama lay at the door, refusing to move, forcing people to step over him. For three days he grieved, along with the rest of the family. On the fourth day he got up, went to Donna and placed his grizzled head in her lap. He had found someone else who needed him.

Today Llama and Donna are rarely separated. They visit neighborhood friends, both dog and human, daily. They go to Guide Dogs meetings, take walks around the lake and occasionally go to the beach. A neighbor has made Llama a ramp so that he can avoid stairs and get in and out of cars. The dog Donna had given a home and her heart to, and then had sent out into the world to help another, had brought that love back to Donna when her need was greatest.

I cried the first time I heard the story of Llama. The second time I heard it, I knew it was a story that needed to be shared. Give yourself to a dog, and you will get love and loyalty in return. Dogs know when you need them most.

Too Many Cats in the Kitchen

Maryellen Burns

Knock! Knock! Knock!!

Six-thirty in the morning! My husband, Leo, and I wake up. Someone's incessantly knocking on the door downstairs. I panic. Who is it? A loved one had an accident? A neighbor found one of our cats dead in the street? I try to shake off my anxiety and the five cats that had rooted themselves to my lap and legs all night.

We stumble to the door. My friend Angela is there. "I'm sorry to come over so early," she says, "but I'm supposed to shoot a commercial for Safeway grocers at seven-thirty and my scheduled location is kaput. You have such a wonderful kitchen. Could I possibly bring a film crew here in an hour?" Her British accent adds an extra note to this early morning request.

My first thoughts are, *Leo has to teach and the*

kitchen is a mess. We haven't cleaned up from dinner last night. Piles of dishes are in the sink and on the stove. We'd need to hide cat bowls and kitty litter, and vacuum up *mucho* cat hair.

Second thought? *Yes!* We spent two years restoring our kitchen and are proud of its 1910 Craftsman features: a six-burner, double-oven Magic Chef range, lush redwood-veneer cabinets, a black-and-white soda-fountain floor and old-fashioned comfiness.

We look at each other. A lot needs to get done. Leo rushes to the kitchen to feed cats, clean and make coffee before dressing and going to work, while I attempt to de-cat the living room.

An hour or so later a crew of eight gathers on the front porch—producer Angela; three men with camera gear; Rosa Nosa, our fluffy tortoiseshell, who has rushed out to greet them; and three outdoor cats, who scramble to hide.

Opening the front door is a struggle because Nishan, our little disabled, back-legs-all-tangled-in-on-themselves cat, is parked in front of it.

I finally get the door open, and a sullen-voiced man, the director, asks, "How many damn cats do you have?"

"Nine," I tell him. "Or possibly more. You never know who they brought home last night."

"There aren't going to be any cats in the kitchen, right?" he asks.

I assure him that the kitchen can be shut off from the rest of the house and it won't be a problem.

Brushing cats away from his legs, he hurries through the living room and into the kitchen, as if he knows the way.

"We need to set up. No time for niceties," he says.

I follow him, and there is Rosa, sitting on the butcher-block island, looking every bit the superb hostess she is.

He picks her up and plops her roughly to the floor. "I said no cats in the kitchen!"

I pick her up, reassure her and take her outside.

"What have you done? Angela said your kitchen had a slightly messy, warm, lived-in look. You've cleaned it. Now we'll have to dirty it again!"

Angela and I look at each other. I can tell that this guy is a major pain in the neck, and I hope I can get through a whole day with him in my house. He gives the room a cursory look.

"I like the stove. I want a pot of water, steam rising from it. Mess up the counters. I want fresh vegetables, canned tomatoes, a flour sack spilling out. Move the butcher block to the center of the room. It should be the focal point. What's that cat doing here? I thought I told you to remove *all* the cats!"

Angela picks up the cat. It's Rosa Nosa again. She starts to purr, presses her red nose against Angela's face. Meanwhile, Hephzibah and Honky, the two oldest cats in the household, wander in, looking for food and water. They jump up on the kitchen table, demanding attention.

For the first time, the director spots Nishan hiding under the kitchen table. She scurries out, dragging her useless hind legs. The director looks disgusted. "What is it with these cats? Get. Them. Out. Of. The. Kitchen. Now!"

"Oh, Terry," pleads Angela. "The talent won't be here for an hour. Let the cats be. We'll clear them out before we start filming."

He looks as if he might relent, but something in the tone of his voice spooks the cats. *This is not a cat person.* They scatter. Except for Rosa, who insists on taking up residence beneath the butcher block with Nishan, her shadow.

To understand Rosa and Nishan's relationship, you need to know a little about how we came to keep them. Rosa was born about three months after my mother died, one of six kittens from Little Guy, Mom's faithful companion throughout her illness. Of all the kittens she was the prettiest, the liveliest, a furry lump of playfulness with an air of responsibility, a dignified poise and a beautiful red patch across her cute little nose. Everything about her reminded us of my mother, Rose. We wanted to keep her but couldn't justify it, because she had so many offers of a home and we had so many kittens to place. We gave her to Monica, a little girl who lived down the street.

Within twenty-four hours, Monica was on our doorstep, a squirming kitten in hand, face and cheeks swollen and red. She was allergic. Would we keep her until she could give her to a new home on Monday? My mother had always said she'd return one day as a madam of a cathouse or as one of Leo's cats. There was a reason this cat had come back to us. We were meant to keep her.

A year later Rosa and Giselle, a loveable stray we had taken in, bore kittens within a few days of each other. A couple of weeks later Giselle moved her kittens atop a bed in Mom's old room, except for the runt, a tortoiseshell that looked a little like Rosa. Leo picked her up. For the first time we realized she had twisted, deformed hind legs. "I don't know if this one is going to survive," he said, carrying her to Giselle and placing her at a teat. But Giselle rejected her and moved the other kittens again. This happened two or three more times.

Leo is softhearted. He hates to see any little critter suffer. Obviously, Giselle didn't want her. Something had to be done. The next day we took her to our vet.

"If her mother refuses to nurse her, she could die in a couple of days on her own, but she looks like a survivor to me. It's a big responsibility, but why don't you try again? You could feed her by hand, and in a week or two we could put a cast on her legs and try to straighten them."

Home she went. Giselle wouldn't nurse her. That night she moved the others yet again. Next morning we're lying in bed. Rosa is nursing her kittens under our desk. We see a little face peeking in at the foot of the doorway and then watch the disabled kitten scurry across the floor to Rosa and push all the other kittens out of the way, looking for sustenance. Rosa begins licking Nishan all over and looks up at us as if to say, "What's one more?"

When almost all the kittens had new homes, my niece Penny showed up with six more, barely three weeks old. Someone had abandoned them. Would Rosa nurse them? Rosa didn't hesitate. All kittens were welcome, but Nishan was her favorite. She never grew beyond the size of an eight-week-old kitten. Rosa continued to nurse Nishan for almost two years. Wherever Rosa went, Nishan followed.

They are together now, watching the crew ready the kitchen for filming. The actors arrive. Rosa runs to the door to greet them and lead them into the kitchen.

Everything is ready for the first take. Spaghetti pot boiling on the stove, lettuce washed and dried by hand, husband and wife intimately touching shoulders as they laugh and make dinner together.

"Cut! Where did that damn cat come from?"

There is Rosa, perched majestically on the lower deck of the butcher block, taking a keen interest in the proceedings. I pick her up and put her on the back porch.

The director sets up the shot again. "Camera's rolling," he says.

The salad is being tossed; noodles are placed in boiling water. I see Nishan, who had remained hidden, peer out from behind a butcher-block leg. Within minutes Rosa is back in place, following every move of the camera. The director doesn't seem to notice at first. When he does, he silently picks her up by the scruff of her neck and tosses her out.

Minutes later she is back, arching her back against the director's legs, as if trying to seduce him. Again, he picks her up and tosses her out the French doors.

Before you know it, she's back again, under the stairs. Neither the director nor the crew has noticed there is a cat door. As I wonder if I should block it so Rosa can't get back in, she suddenly leaps from the floor to the kitchen table and then takes another flight to the butcher block.

"There are too many cats in the kitchen!" the director barks and stomps out of the room.

Angela follows him. I hear muffled voices, his strident and nasty, Angela's soft and lilting as she tries to calm him. One actor has picked Rosa up and is tickling her under her chin. She responds with a rumbling purr and a gracious movement of her head.

The director comes back, temper under control, but

barely. Angela follows, a catlike smile on her face. "A few more takes and we're done," he says. "I give up."

Rosa remained in place for the rest of the morning, looking like Gloria Swanson in *Sunset Boulevard* demanding her close-up.

"That's a wrap," the director called.

He never broke a smile or thanked us for giving up our house and our time. He just watched silently as the rest of the crew packed up the camera gear, the lights, the food, petted Rosa one more time and left.

A week or so later Angela called to say that the commercial was going to air at 6:00 p.m. on Tuesday and would be rebroadcast for a month or two.

We set up the television recorder, gathered all the cats on the bed and waited to see Rosa's debut. The commercial ended. The editor had left all Rosa's scenes on the cutting room floor! The ad was okay but we thought it lacked the emotional punch Rosa might have given it.

Rosa, in one of her rare acts of petulance, jumped off the bed. In solidarity the other cats followed her. Only Nishan remained to ease our disappointment. A strong union household, we boycotted Safeway for a while but realized it wasn't their call; it was the call of a director who didn't realize that the biggest joy of all is too many cats in the kitchen.

Transforming U

Suzanne Tomlinson

As a longtime journalist, I never imagined a writing assignment from a popular horse magazine would lead me to personal transformation. But that was exactly what happened when I met a horse with a giant letter *U* branded on his well-muscled neck.

I'd been asked to write a piece about how to have a successful match when adopting a horse from a rescue center. A lifelong horse-crazy gal with horses of my own, I was excited about the assignment.

I interviewed the Grace Foundation director, Beth DeCaprio. She provided some solid information and great tips on how to find a perfect equine partner at a rescue organization. Then she told me about an upcoming project —the HELP Rescue Me Trainers' Showcase. It had grown out of a crisis involving wild horses.

In the Midwest about two hundred of the Bureau

of Land Management's mustangs had gone through three auctions with no bidders. When that happens, the BLM brands the horses nobody wants with a big letter *U* to identify them as unwanted. They are no longer the responsibility of the BLM. Most of the horses with this sad scarlet letter go to slaughter operators. These particular two hundred *U* horses were sent to a ranch in Nebraska, where a rancher placed them on his property and then left them to fend for themselves.

The Humane Society of the United States rushed in to help but not before many of these horses died from starvation. Horse rescue groups, including the Grace Foundation, traveled to a rehab center where the surviving mustangs were being held in the hopes that they could be helped. Beth and her volunteers agreed to take thirty-one of the *U* horses back to her center in California, near Sacramento. Other rescue organizations took on the remaining unwanted horses.

Beth came home with the daunting task of finding these horses forever homes. Suddenly an inspiration hit her. Why not pair professional trainers with each of her thirty-one mustangs to give these wild horses seventy days of training and make them more adoptable?

Local trainers took to the idea. They came to the Grace Foundation and each picked out a mustang. At the end of the training period Beth brought the whole gang—mustangs and their trainers—to the big annual horse expo in Sacramento to show off. She called it the Trainers' Showcase. Each trainer demonstrated to the crowd what had been accomplished in those seventy days of training. I watched in the audience as thirty-one horses and thirty-one trainers entered the arena to show what an untrained wild horse could learn in a very short time. The crowd in the stands was moved to standing ovations again and again. Many of the horses were under saddle and seemed at ease with the chaos of the arena, the lights and the noisy crowd. Some of the U-branded horses had learned impressive dressage movements; others jumped obstacles with confidence; all had the beginnings of trust with humans, despite the fact that all the humans they'd met in the past had brought them nothing but hardship and pain. At the end of the event the mustangs were offered for adoption. Would they still be unwanted?

I wrote my story about adopting a horse from a rescue organization, plus a sidebar about the unwanted horses at the horse expo. Editors at the magazine suggested I check on the U-branded horses in a few months and find out what had happened to them.

In the meantime my life suddenly, unexpectedly, turned upside down. My seemingly solid twenty-four-year marriage crumbled, damaged beyond repair. For a time I thought the shock and the pain would kill me. I fled to the guesthouse on our property to be alone.

In those first few days of facing the ugly truth about a marriage I had thought was based on faithfulness, I asked God for help. I remember praying, *Dear God, if what I feel now is going to kill me, please take me now. But if I am supposed to survive it, please let me rest and feel your peace. Show me your light and I will know I can get through this.*

For the first time in several days I slept for many hours. What awakened me was not the jolting remembrance of the nightmare I was living. It was the brightest light of morning I had ever seen, streaming through window blinds that were closed...the light so bright, so lovingly piercing, it woke me up. Something had shifted in that dark night of the soul. In the recesses of my mind there was a knowing—*I am deeply loved by God and the divine that dwells within me.* The pain, the anger, the unbearable grief just dissolved away. God's peace was all around me and in me. *Thank you, God,* I said to myself. *I have my answer. I can go on.*

In the days that followed I began to count my blessings. Our children were grown and on their own. I had financial resources. And I had strength beyond anything I could have imagined. Upon filing for divorce, I moved out. I found a nice house on five acres with a perfect setup for horses and moved in, along with two dogs, one cat and my two horses.

Complete healing would take some time, but I was

no longer afraid to face the truth. I also knew I had to plumb the depths of my own emotions to try and understand why I had been burned by the scorched earth of betrayal time and time again throughout my life.

I thought of the *U*-branded horses and realized, though I didn't carry that letter outwardly, I carried it inwardly. To most people, and even to myself on a conscious level, I was a happy, optimistic, career-driven woman with lots of love in my life. I had children I adored and many relationships I treasured. But I had been drawn to men who seemed to love me on one level and hate me on another. I would start out with the warm glow of feeling cherished. But invariably over time the relationships brought a cold, sad message—I was unwanted.

My mother delivered that scarlet letter *U* for "unwanted" when I was just a girl. She was a troubled person, depressed and addicted to alcohol, which further twisted her mind. Underneath it all, there was always a spark of meanness. I tried to steer clear of her sting and just let it drift past, but the day came when her darkness changed my life.

I don't remember what I asked of her. It could have been a ride to a friend's house. I know it wasn't much. She sneered at me, a suspicious, small smile curling her lips. Already I was on alert. *Nothing good is going to come out of her mouth,* I thought.

She said, "Suzanne, dear, you are such a lucky girl, aren't you? You've had the security and safety of feeling loved all your young life, haven't you?"

Why is she saying these things to me? There is something sinister brewing.

"Yes, poor dear, the truth will confuse you, but here it is. I have never loved you, never wanted you, never cherished you. You are unloved."

People underestimate the power of words. These words, her words, devastated me. It was the deepest betrayal from mother to daughter—an intentional fire set to burn down the trust of an innocent, unsuspecting child.

Looking back over my life, I think my mother loved me. I also think she very much wanted to hurt me. It's hard to reconcile those feelings and actions—loving and hurting seem so discordant. But I have come to understand that her desire to hurt must have derived from some deep wound of her own. Over the years and after her death from the effects of alcoholism, I thought I had forgiven her. What I didn't know was that I carried that wound of her words deep in my subconscious mind, and it colored my opinion of myself. Unwanted. Unloved.

Again I had walked into the fire of someone else's

loving and hurting. Had I stayed married to a man for twenty-four years because in my subconscious he replayed my mother's themes?

I had to try and heal this deep hurt, or I was destined to invite betrayal into my life for unlimited visits. But how to heal? How to forgive? That seemed like a tall order. There was another way to keep betrayal from my door and it seemed easier. *Just never love again,* I thought. For a short while that seemed like the best answer. Then I met the plain brown horse with the big *U* on his neck.

I had checked back on the unwanted mustangs from the Grace Foundation's Trainers' Showcase. There on the website I found a listing of the *U*-branded horses. As I scrolled down, I could see in bold letters next to their names the word "adopted"! It was exciting to see that so many of these most unwanted of the unwanted had found forever homes—except one horse, at the bottom of the list. They called him Vigilant. He was a plain brown ten-year-old mustang with a sturdy-looking body and a kind eye. The vet had noted that he had been gelded and was healthy, with no apparent problems other than the trust issues that went along with being severely neglected. There was no happy, bold "adopted" next to this horse's name.

I wanted this unwanted horse. It just felt right to start my new life wanting the unwanted. It would help remind that little girl who resided in my subconscious, she was wanted and loved very deeply. I made a promise to bring that kind of sacred love to my life in any way I could. I had rescued two abandoned dogs, so why not this horse? And this is how Vigilant found his forever home with me. I spoke with the trainer who had worked with him, and she told me that he had a willing attitude but definitely did not offer automatic trust to all who approached. She suggested I start all over again in his training...being careful to first establish that trust.

And so the two U-branded souls began their work together. The first week I fed him only over the fence and let him settle into his new space next to my other two horses. He didn't seem nervous but I could tell he was wary. The second week I went into his pasture and tried to approach. He ran from me each time. I didn't try to catch him. I just stood as near as he would let me and talked to him softly.

And then like a tightly closed bud protecting itself from winter's frost, the horse, like the flower, began to open to me. He let me approach and stroke his neck, moving my hand over that awful U, wishing I could erase it. The following week, when I opened his pasture gate, he trotted over to me, inviting me to pat him. When it seemed time to put a halter on, he lowered his head into it willingly.

Still, I moved very slowly with him—one little

success at a time. In a month I thought he was ready for some round pen work on a lunge line. I discovered that wonderful foundation the first trainer had established. This horse followed my commands perfectly when I asked him to walk, trot, stop and then move out again. When I asked for the canter, it was clear he had no idea what I wanted, but he tried, anyway, trotting ever faster as I urged him to move out. I changed my communication style. Instead of using my voice to ask for this faster gait, I moved my own legs to the cadence of the canter.

Now he was really confused. I could sense what he was thinking. *You want me to run? But mostly I run when I'm fleeing something threatening. Are you scary?* How could I tell him I didn't want him to run in fear? I wanted him to run in a new way, slower, more controlled, a dance I might one day join him in. I talked to him softly, moving my feet to show him what I wanted, and when he began to gallop too fast, I said encouragingly, "Good boy! Now just slow it down a bit."

One day I just thought, *It's time to get on this horse.* Moving things along very slowly, I put my foot in the stirrup and stepped up to the saddle, then down again. He was so quiet. In a few days I felt sure enough of him to put my foot in the stirrup and swing all the way up and into the saddle. I asked him with my legs and my voice to move out at a walk. He responded perfectly.

And what a perfect moment for me. *Never trust, never love again?* This horse had been abused, neglected and betrayed, yet he was showing me *he* was willing to trust again. Who was *I* to shut out the world? If I could build mutual trust with this horse, building it with a human being might be possible. This horse was showing me the way. I would be open to love again someday and then I would know how. *Just take it slow. Build it step by step. Be wary, but be willing.*

I thought back to that moment of deep self-love in my dark night of the soul. That love was a bridge to freedom—freedom from anger, sadness, regret, self-recrimination...freedom to be wholly and holy loved. Now riding this *U*-branded horse, I reached down and stroked his neck. "You are not unwanted and will never again be unwanted. I want you. You are loved." The horse and I had stepped up to our challenges. I was healing that *U* brand in my soul. I would not be a slave to betrayal.

My plain brown horse deserved a name that would transform that sad *U* into something fitting his grandness. Why not *U*nderestimated and *U*ltimately free? Now I open his pasture gate and call his new name. "Good morning, Freedom!" He calls back with a whinny and trots to my side.

A Nose for Love

Dena Kouremetis

When my husband, George, and I look back, we shake our heads in disbelief. We didn't find one another on a dating site or throw flirtations to one another across a crowded bar. The brother of my maid of honor, George was a groomsman in my 1982 wedding to someone else.

See, it's a Greek thing. During the ensuing twenty years, I'd spot George at Greek weddings, festivals, funerals, picnics and dances I would attend with my husband. And each time I'd see him, I would ask his sister about him, taking curious note of the fact that he'd stayed single. My knowledge of George extended to his being a gregarious, good-looking family friend that danced well. After my marriage broke up two decades later, however, I was to discover that George was still there, unattached. And when he found out I was about to become single myself, he wasted no time saying he had no intention of missing his chance to finally get to know me. Well, it's just about the most flattering thing a middle-aged woman can have happen to her, isn't it?

So is *this* what they meant by "happily ever after?" Well, almost.

You see, my new love made it clear early on that he had pet allergies and that, although he liked dogs, he would probably never own one. *Pet dander* was a new term to me.

"What happens when you're around a dog?" I asked.

A pained look came over George's face. "My sinuses get stuffed up and I get headaches. Then I get sinus infections and it's awful."

Hmm, really? I'd had small dogs throughout my life. They'd warmed my lap, watched TV with me, melted me with their doleful eyes and filled up spaces in my heart humans simply couldn't. It was tough to face the idea of never owning one again. "Can't you get shots?" I asked.

George looked at me as if I had reduced his affliction to inoculating livestock, and it was there the subject ended.

As things got more serious between us, I rationalized the idea of having the freedom to travel and socialize without worrying about a pet. I could accidentally drop food on the floor or leave a door open without having to worry about a little being scurrying to snatch up the morsel or run out of the house. The freedom began to grow on me. A little.

The day finally came when my daughter walked me down the aisle to George and life began anew. At dinner with some friends not long after we moved into our new home, we learned they were getting a Shima puppy flown down from the Northwest—a shih tzu–Maltese crossbreed, a dog that had become popular over the past few years for its personality, its no-shed fur and, of course, its cuteness factor. Rena and her daughters would excitedly show us photos of their mail-order dog. There was jubilation the day Maxie's doggy crate, containing a floppy-eared, mop-tailed pup, was handed to its new owners at the Sacramento airport. In the end, Maxie would be everything this little family had wanted in a dog and more. He was adorable, easy to train, smart and absolutely charming. Even people who hated most dogs loved this little guy.

Rena could tell I was smitten with her new four-legged charge. I'd make any excuse to "stop by" for a visit and I loved it when she or her girls would knock on our door with Maxie in tow. And even though I'd watch George begin to sniffle afterward, it was apparent that he became putty in Maxie's paws. Soon a conspiracy began to hatch. Rena began forwarding me by email photos of new Shima puppies she received from the Spokane, Washington, breeder of her own pup.

The short-limbed, big-eyed blobs of fur in the photos were, of course, totally disarming. The pure white ones looked like tiny snowy owls, and the brown ones like diminutive shaggy dogs you could cuddle to death, like the character in Steinbeck's *Of Mice and Men,* if you weren't careful. With each set of photos I forwarded to George, he'd make a remark that I was trying to wear him down. I was. By the time I forwarded the third batch of litter photos to George, it was all over.

"Did you see the black-and-white one?" he calls to me as we occupy our respective home offices in our new house.

"Oh, yeah. He's my favorite," I admit.

A few minutes go by. I hear nothing but the click of George's mouse. Then a feeble voice echoes down the hall to me. "I think we have to go see this little guy."

If I could do a happy dance atop my Aeron chair without killing myself, I would have risked looking like an idiot.

Before he could change his mind, I was busy emailing the breeder, asking questions about the black-furred, roly-poly handful with the white paws and white belly. She told us about his parents, how he was the first puppy that wanted to be held, how large he might grow (no more than eight to ten pounds) and when he would turn eight weeks old—just old enough for him to leave his mama. The next day, knowing our heightened interest level, the breeder snapped more photos of him and sent them hurling through cyberspace. There was one of him standing on her deck, one with him shakily perched atop a rock and another one that was a close-up of his little black-and-white face. We were head over heels in love with our small furry Internet date.

Our minds began racing. Recently we had won the grand prize from a raffle George had entered—a free cruise for two to Alaska. The ship was to leave from and return to Seattle, only one hundred miles from where the breeder lived. So instead of flying, we schemed to take a few extra days and drive up so we could swing by and collect our tiny live cargo.

There was much to do to prepare for a new arrival in our house. As we wandered the aisles of the local big-box pet store before the trip, it was as if we were a couple shopping for baby things. We collected books, talked to on-site trainers and bought tiny puppy toys, not knowing what our new puppy might like. At home, we scoured the Internet for information on bringing a puppy home and found that things had indeed changed since I had owned my last dog. Using crates had become the preferred method of house training, since they emulated the security of the place puppies were born. I had even seen *Dog Whisperer* on TV, a series showing people how to train their puppies without resorting to scaring them by using rolled-up newspapers. It was all about understanding how dogs think and not attributing human characteristics to them. I looked forward to using all the newer techniques with this little guy.

The drive to Seattle was fun and the cruise was glorious. But when we got off the cruise ship and reclaimed our car, it was all about the puppy, which we had already named Cosmo, for his cosmopolitan-looking tuxedo markings. After several hours of scenic driving, we stood at the front door of the breeder's house like two parents-to-be at an orphanage, waiting to see the child we had received only pictures of. The breeder and her husband were gracious, friendly people with several litters for sale—two Shima litters and a passel of Yorkshire terriers, all of whom looked like tiny *Monopoly* tokens, fully proportioned from head to toe. And then we spotted him. Cosmo looked up at us, wagging his entire body, just before his older brother jumped him from behind. There was no doubt that of the entire gang romping before us, this was the little man of our Internet dreams.

We were ushered into the backyard to watch the toddlers romp in order to see more of his personality. His mom was out there, too, still correcting her pups by occasionally "scruffing" a neck or two. And what personality…Cosmo jumped with his siblings, squatted to take a tiny leak and then, ignoring his playmates, began crawling on top of George as he sat on the grass at puppy level. If this had been a real estate deal, George would have signed all the paperwork and handed over the check before knowing anything more about the property. It was love at first cuddle.

Cosmo is now a two-year-old, incredibly cute member of our household. He greets us every morning as if we had been gone for months and makes our entire day complete before it has even started. It's Cosmic bliss as our little friend licks our feet, nuzzles our necks and heaves big sighs of contentment.

So what happened to the allergies George claimed he had? Yes, he has them. But he makes this doggy relationship work, just as he makes ours work—with love, patience, compromise, understanding and the occasional antihistamine. I like to think of our lives with Cosmo as a three-way love affair of sorts—the happy ending to a warm, fuzzy fairy tale, just as special as the one about how George magically changed his role in my life from groomsman to bridegroom in thirty short years.

Mother Knows Best

Kathryn Canan

I peered out the bathhouse window from behind the faded yellow-polka-dotted curtains. It wasn't safe yet; they were still out there. Perhaps if I peeked out the door and made a bit of noise, I'd be able to scare them off. I opened the door a few inches; it scraped on the uneven concrete floor, and the hinges squealed. Slowly I closed it again and then opened it, drawing out the unearthly sounds. I tried banging the door and shouting, to no avail.

Mama Moose was totally wrapped up in showing her baby where the best-tasting flowers and shrubs were growing. I wasn't going to take a chance that she would trust me walking past them to get back up the hill to our cabin. Few animals are more dangerous than a moose defending her calf—I had as much respect for her as I would for a grizzly. I'd seen enough reports in Montana newspapers about people who hadn't learned that lesson.

Since I had no real choice, I decided to relax and enjoy the sight, although it was clear Mama wasn't going to win any beauty contests. Bull moose (or male moose) are majestic, but cows (or female moose) can easily be mistaken for awkward, malnourished horses with strange ears and knobby knees. The calf had not yet outgrown its reddish-brown coat; he or she had just been born that spring and would stay with its mother for at least a year.

Our house is what decorating magazines call "rustic." Normally it's not a problem having no bathroom in the cabin. It started life as a small log cabin on an old dude ranch in the 1920s. Previous owners had added a kitchen and a porch and had brought in running water from a nearby creek. My parents, who bought the cabin in 1961, when I was still in diapers, had added electricity but had balked at digging a septic tank. The common bathhouse for the old dude ranch was fifty yards down the hill. A bathroom so far away has its advantages, though. The stars are incredible on a clear night at three in the morning.

Moose, thank goodness, are not nocturnal, so we're usually safe on those midnight treks. We tend to see them in the morning and evening, stopping at what used to be a salt lick behind our cabin, on the way to or from the creek. Recently the Forest Service informed us that "baiting" animals with salt blocks is illegal, even though there had been one on a stump outside the back window for at least eighty years. No matter...the stump is saturated with salt by now and the moose come, anyway. Trouble is, they seem to have gone nuts this year and invaded Camp Senia.

I can hardly blame them. It probably feels like the only safe haven for miles around. Mother Nature went on a rampage a couple of years ago, with gusts of wind up over one hundred miles per hour, which felled lodgepole pines all over the forest. Perhaps it was nature's way of clearing out the pine bark beetles killing her trees. As if the windstorm didn't do enough damage, along came a drought and a bolt of lightning the next summer to finish the cleanup. Fire.

I had an excellent view of the first cloud of smoke from that fire, since I was four miles up the side of the canyon, enjoying the pristine blue sky reflected in Timberline Lake. I don't know where the moose went when that fire hit, but I got myself down the mountain faster than I ever thought possible, grabbed my car keys and drove the twelve miles out of the canyon with the firestorm just behind me and moving fast. I passed firefighters heading up and hoped sincerely that no one would be hurt defending our cabin.

Our cabin neighbors had forced my mother into

their car at the first sign of fire. After we reunited in town, we spent a sleepless night and the next day huddled in anxious mourning. Finally, my mother got the call from our friendly forest ranger. Owing to the luck of the wind (and relentless nagging by said forest ranger to create defensible space), twenty of the twenty-five cabins in Camp Senia were spared, and we lost only our woodpile.

To fight this huge forest fire, firefighters worked for the next three months, until the October snows put out the last of the fire. By the time the fire was stopped, it had covered a huge distance, eight miles east down the canyon and three miles to the west from its origin; both sides of the canyon were devastated up to the timberline.

Camp Senia, then, was left as a little island of green surrounded by a seemingly lifeless, charred skeleton. When we returned the following summer, we could see gleaming granite boulders previously hidden by dense undergrowth sitting starkly on the mountainside. Piles of chips, where the rocks had peeled from the intense heat, lay underneath them.

Not everything was black; the first summer after the fire already tiny ribbons of green were beginning to grow along the small streams running down the canyon sides to the main creek near the cabin. It seemed that these little trails were all pointing toward our miraculously saved haven.

So the moose came.

They came to the meadows dotted with blue penstemon flowers, which were already obliterating the sites of the burned cabins. They nibbled tender fir trees and the young shoots of shrubs whose roots had survived the fire. A venerable bull moose reclaimed his kingdom on the islands formed where the creek slows down and widens out, while members of his harem basked in the sun behind our cabin, on a patch of kinnikinnick, a plant that is an evergreen ground cover.

The moose and other animals give back to nature as much as they consume; along with the ash from the fire, they fertilize the new growth. Each summer since the fire, the forest has been blanketed with wildflowers—a varied palette of paintbrush, mountain bluebells, bright yellow balsamroot, orange and yellow monkey flowers, and the blooming promise of berries that ripen sooner in sunnier meadows. The flowers give shelter to new seedlings of lodgepole pine, a species whose cones open only in response to the intense heat of a fire.

At last I watched Mama Moose lead her calf down past the lodge, where guests of the dude ranch used to enjoy Western barbecues. The moose were heading for their own banquet of tender plants growing in the creek, washed down by fresh snowmelt. It was now safe for me to leave the bathroom and head back up the hill to the cabin. Closing the door quietly behind me,

I waved toward the moose and sent them a wordless thank-you. A thank-you for reminding me of the natural wonders that have resulted from what had seemed to me, as a cabin owner, like utter devastation.

Spotty's Miracle

Charles Kuhn

He came to us as a gift, not asked for or expected. A little bundle of dappled tan-and-black fur accented with black spots. Hence, we named him Spotty. His huge ears made him look like a very small bunny rather than a young puppy whose owner wasn't able to care for a disabled pet.

My wife, Melissa, a schoolteacher, was an easy mark. She has a soft spot for animals and seldom turns an injured or sick animal away. I was an even easier mark. My struggle with progressive multiple sclerosis keeps me home and makes me particularly empathetic to animals with disabilities. So I became Spotty's full-time caregiver.

He weighed in at two pounds. His sweet disposition made you love him from the moment you met him. His eyes trapped your heart, two shining brown orbs that stared up at you in complete innocence. Who could resist that look? We sure couldn't.

His back legs didn't work. I could relate to Spotty's discomfort, having slowly lost most of the use of my own legs. Spotty would never race with the other dogs. I may never toss a football or play golf again.

We hoped his condition might be due to poor nutrition and corrected his diet. He gained a few ounces and, with careful muscle massages and flexion, soon scrambled across the floor. But his limited motor skills never allowed him to walk properly or play with our other dogs. We carried him everywhere—often from the couch to my desk chair, where he slept on my lap in cozy luxury throughout the day, snuggled in the comfort of his favorite blanket. At night he was cradled between us, swaddled up to prevent any bladder accidents. He never heard a disparaging word. Through no fault of his own, his handicapped life offered him enough challenge. We never burdened him with more.

We scheduled a veterinarian appointment for a general health checkup and to see if any light could be cast on his condition. Some sort of neurological disorder was suspected, but the diagnosis went no further. Our daily routine with Spotty continued, until one evening everything changed.

Melissa was in the backyard on a rainy evening, filling feed trays in the aviary. Spotty lay on my lap as we enjoyed our time together on the couch, but as he was prone to do, he stretched his back legs aggressively and propelled himself from my lap onto the cushion next to me. I quickly righted him, but something was terribly wrong. He gulped for air. The color of his gums turned from pink to blue to white. I put my pinkie finger down his throat, thinking he may have swallowed a thread from my sweater or a piece of lint. I turned him upside down and patted his back in a silly effort to perform a doggy Heimlich maneuver. Nothing worked. I grabbed my cell phone and dialed Melissa, screaming at her to get in the house. Within moments she burst in the front room.

I yelled, "It's Spotty! He's dying!" She ran to me, grabbed him and headed out the door. She was gone with Spotty. I didn't even have a chance to say goodbye.

I listened to the rain pelt the roof and said a silent prayer for my wife to drive safely and for Spotty's life. Melissa told me later that she drove like a maniac to the veterinarian's office, steering the car down the rain-soaked pavement as she performed mouth-to-nose resuscitation to keep Spotty alive.

She ran into the veterinarian's office, screaming at the top of her lungs. The doctor jumped into action to save Spotty. After nearly ten minutes of not having a heartbeat or a breath, Spotty came back. The cause of this emergency was unknown. At the time we didn't care. This little angel that had fallen into our lives lived again. Ecstatic, we'd worry about the cause later. For now we had our little miracle back with us.

"Later" came in about sixty days. We had been referred to a very reputable veterinary school in a nearby community. Using high-optic X-ray technology, the doctor soon diagnosed luxating cervical vertebrae in his neck. Any awkward movement that dropped Spotty's chin to his chest could result in his spinal cord being pinched by misaligned vertebrae, which would cut off necessary nerve impulses to keep his heart and lungs working. A surgical correction was dangerous and economically unrealistic. We were told that a do-not-resuscitate order should be followed at his next seizure.

It became our goal to treat every second of the remainder of his life as a gift and to relish the joy of his presence. Each moment of his resurrection was cherished. A month after his diagnosis, tragedy struck. Spotty had been cradled with extreme care every day since we were made aware of his prognosis, carried in a small flat bed with cushioned and slightly elevated edges to prop his head up. We snuck him into the movie theater. We carried him into stores, where one kind shopper saw his ears and commented, "What a cute bunny."

Then, one night, his exuberance took him. He propelled himself aggressively into the corner of his bed, where his neck bent down and the misaligned vertebrae squeezed his spinal cord. In that second the damage was done. My wife tried valiantly to revive him. We lost our precious Spotty that night. Melissa sobbed uncontrollably.

We were devastated. I blamed myself for taking my eyes off him. Melissa was inconsolable. We slept little that night. The next day Melissa dutifully showed up to teach her fifth-grade class. She stifled sobs throughout the day.

On her lunch break Melissa called the teacher's assistant who'd brought Spotty into our lives and told her what had happened. Later that afternoon the woman came to the door of Melissa's classroom with a small puppy. Spotty's twin sister, Sophie. She hadn't told Melissa she had kept Spotty's sister. She didn't think Spotty would live out his life, and she'd planned to give Sophie to Melissa when that sad day came.

When Melissa came home that evening and walked into my office, holding a little spotted puppy with bunny ears, I was dumbstruck. Another miracle had occurred. Spotty had been brought back to us a second time! But that wasn't the fact. Melissa introduced me to Sophie.

Spotty can never be replaced, but Sophie has helped mend the tear in our hearts from losing him. We will never forget Spotty. His incurable zest for life was an inspiration to anyone, but especially to me. When you are helpless to stop a disease that ravages your body, it's easy to feel sorry for yourself. I'm six-two, but I found encouragement from a two-pound puppy. Between us, Spotty and I didn't have a decent pair of legs. I could relate. Another way I feel even closer to Spotty is by remembering that he and I both came into this world with healthy twin sisters, who deliver miracles by their sheer presence on a daily basis. He had Sophie. I have my twin sister, Judy. A miracle to be cherished each and every day.

Sophie will never take Spotty's place. But she has created her own place in our hearts. There are times when I cuddle Sophie and look into her innocent, loving eyes and thank her for bringing such joy into our hearts and for helping me recall her precious brother, Spotty. He will never be forgotten and his memory will always be cherished. She reminds me of that wonderful gift each moment I hold her close to my heart, and I quietly offer my thanks for twins.

The Nursery

Robyn Boyer

The birds started showing up around the same time I was ready to throw in the towel.

My house, my job, my life were coming apart at the seams. My home, purchased post-divorce, so carefully styled into a beautiful, welcoming and feng shui–perfect haven, had become a burden. The maintenance costs and challenges were eating at my savings, my strength and my nerves.

The breaking point came when, out of the blue and for no apparent reason, the sliding-glass door between the living room and the smaller of my two enclosed brick patios spontaneously shattered into a thousand pieces. No errant BB shot, no thrown rock from a passing kid or truck, no explanation except maybe poltergeists. This came on the heels of having to shell out thousands of dollars to replace cracked and uplifted sections of my driveway, caused by a tree planted by the developer years ago in the too-narrow strip between my drive and the neighbor's.

The homeowners' association had also begun to hassle me about the house's unsightly rust-stained rain gutters and trim. My house, built by the developer as a showpiece and to sell lots for big custom homes around a man-made lake, also still had the original roof. That was twenty-two years ago, and there was only so much you could do once the shakes started cracking and curling in the relentless Sacramento summers and shedding after every winter storm. A house of woes.

So there I was, with no more savings, trudging back and forth each day to an underpaid, soul-bleaching job, my health and well-being a crapshoot. When the glass door cracked, I did, too. Sobbing, overwhelmed and bone-weary from the seemingly endless struggle to keep going, I sent an email to my father and a few friends. I see now that it was a cry for help, something I'm not too fond of doing, but there it was: fall into the abyss or ask for a hand.

My father responded by sending me a Wikipedia link explaining why windows sometimes spontaneously break. Another friend said, "I don't know what to say." But my friend Gail, my rock, my beacon, said, "Hold on. You're not going anywhere. I've got your back."

She's a cop, and I could hear her commanding voice through the email.

The solution was to sell the house, rent and get out from under burdens too great to bear. Bit by bit, with Gail's support and assistance, I made my way, worrying as I have all my life that this, too, would fall away, pulled out from under me at the most inconvenient time. On the edge, never safe, always on the edge. My close companions Depression and its good friend Anxiety love the edge. They work there to cloud your sense of direction, twine themselves around your heart like a gnarly root, take hold and squeeze the life out of you if you don't chop at them with whatever tools you've got. Worst of all, they rob you of your sense of what is possible.

I put the house on the godforsaken market, which was still teetering from the international financial meltdown, replaced the sliding-glass door and more sections of the concrete driveway, and had the gutters and trim repaired and painted. Now all I had to do was come to terms with a buyer and the unsettling proposition of moving my life's accumulation of stuff— pushed in one direction by pragmatism and pulled in another by attachment.

And that was when I began to notice the birds around my back patio. At first it was just a pair or two. Little common finches, the males dandied up with orange crests and breasts, the females drab brown with white and tan speckles. Sometimes there would be just three of them, two males jockeying for a female. But then they started coming in droves. One pair turned into dozens, with the occasional odd man out. The twitters and calls of a few soon became a din as the scout birds sent word that bird heaven awaited all who arrived.

What had been designed and built to be an outdoor room for entertaining people became transformed over the spring and summer months into a playground and nesting area for the birds. It was like a theme park for finches, with diaper stations and a drinking and splashing fountain. The copper railings I'd installed atop one of the patio walls to espalier the camellia bushes became a singles bar, a place for males and females to land, check each other out, flirt and hook up. A paned mirror with a shelf became a favorite spot to peck away at their own images for hours, leaving a daily mess of droppings on the ledge and sloppy kisses on the glass. The outdoor fan became a tilt-a-whirl as one after another would fly full throttle, land on a blade and ride the spin round and round until it stopped.

They built their nests above the patio, under the roof's eaves, on top of a broad, load-bearing beam. They tucked them back into the *V* where the beam and the overhang intersected. I watched as they swept in throughout the spring days, carrying straw and lint and long pieces of dried plants in their tiny beaks, sometimes squabbling over materials. At one point a pair decided to build a nest atop one of my outdoor speakers attached to the beam. Not sure this was a good thing, I pulled the makings down before they could get to the stage of patching it all together with spit and droppings. I did this three separate times, but the couple persisted, returning each day with a fresh stash of nest material until I relented. *Okay, you win,* I thought. *It's your imperative and the least I can do for all the delight you bring.*

They took over the backs of the patio chairs, a short hop from the fountain and the copper railings and just a quick flight to the nests above. Some days I'd look out and see the tops of four of the six chairs lined with birds, as many as six or seven to a chair. My cat would often lie in one of the chairs, catching a nap in the afternoon sun. The birds ignored her and she ignored them. Everybody felt safe, I guess.

I'd have to clean up the patio on Sundays for open houses, and even though the birds disappeared while I hosed everything down and, presumably, the females laid low in the nests while lookie-loos poked about my place, once all the strangers cleared out and the activity subsided, the birds returned, reclaiming their rightful place in my backyard.

Once the nests were built and the little blue eggs laid, the females brooded and the males kept company and food steadily arriving. One by one, each nest sprang to life with four or five tiny babies. Although the babies were hidden from view and thus well protected from passing predators, like blue jays, if I moved slowly and didn't startle the mothers, I could see the babies from inside my living room as they poked their tiny gray heads up, beaks opened wide, clamoring in a high-pitched keen for food. Mornings and early evenings, when I was home from work, I'd listen to the sounds of life seeking life and smile with gratefulness.

Soon enough the babies grew too big and had to leave the nests. I watched the parents as they weaned their brood, going from feedings several times a day to just perching on the nest with a "Well, what do you want me to do about it?" look when the fledglings peeped for food. *How do they know what to do and when to do it?* I wondered of the parents. Could I learn some primal lesson, apply it to my own role as a parent, see how much was too much to give or just the right amount? The hard-nosed indifference the parents showed at this point in their offspring's development both impressed and disturbed me.

That was when the worrying started. I feared for the babies' safety from jays. I worried that with all the jostling going on in the now too-small nests, one of them would fall out and onto the bricks. I found a dead baby on the ground, in the planter that borders the brick, and wrapped it in a gossamer cloth bag. With a heavy and trepidant heart, I buried it deep in the mounded dirt around the camellia bushes. I worried that the babies might starve because their parents somehow weren't wired right, that maybe they'd been passed over when Nature distributed the familial handbook. I worried that the house wouldn't sell, that I'd never find a better job, that I was blowing it as a parent. Like the fledglings, I was on the precipice of my own future, unsure and scared, but unlike them, I was too wound up to trust my instincts.

One by one the fledglings made their way. I'd see them hopping about, testing their wings with a short flight from the patio's brick pavers to the backs of the chairs. From there they might flutter over to the fountain or into the persimmon tree. The persimmon tree, which was finally starting to bear fruit after three years of leaves and not much more, became a way station for them, a safe place to flutter to and hide before attempting the longer flights to the top of the forty-foot-tall cottonwood tree in the neighbor's yard. I knew the babies were going to be okay when they could fly from the copper railings to the top of that cottonwood. It was the highest perch in the neighborhood. And as with the backs of my chairs, I'd see dozens of them hanging out together there, perched on the arched branches at the very top, swaying with the winds.

When I was lamenting one day the growing absence of the birds, my daughter assured me in her knowing and wise way that my fears for the birds, for her and for myself were misplaced and that everything would work out, take its proper course. "Nature's a bitch, Mom. This patio was a nursery. Be glad you gave them that."

Watching the fledglings become fliers calmed me down and restored my hopes. By summer's end the nests had emptied and my bird park had closed for the season. I had the occasional visitors, probably the babies who, now grown, were starting their own round late in the breeding cycle. The persimmon tree produced so much fruit that it toppled over and had to be culled and restaked. Neighbors living on my street bought my house as an investment and I now rent from them; I didn't even have to move. My job prospects are looking up. I've slimmed down and generally perked up.

When Gail jumped in to help, she asked only one thing of me. Her lifesaving assignment for me was to write down what the next twenty years of my life would look like, in other words, what I wanted from those years. As the challenges that once seemed insurmountable fall away, and I search for answers and a life of purpose, I realize that she has made me feel safe...like the birds must have felt when making my patio their nursery. I'm betting they'll return next year. I'll be here, brimming with a sense of the possible, waiting to see what life will bring.

Frank Observations

E. G. Fabricant

Every dog deserves a boy, or two.

Smooth-haired and black and tan, Frank came to us—to my wife, my two boys, aged ten and approaching eight years, and me—in mid-1985, on the outskirts of Alexandria, Virginia.

His procurement process was equal parts evolutionary and deliberate. My wife, Geri, grew up with miniature dachshunds. I was a dog-deprived child, growing up in a family with eight children; we span twenty-one years from oldest to youngest. My parents' patience with nonathletic, character-building activities—dancing lessons, music lessons and pet ownership—ran out with my next oldest brother. Their tolerance for dogs ran out even sooner. After four different dogs met with sad fates, my mother put her foot down when I was ten. Literally.

"God*damn* it, Frank! *I'm* not feeding, walking and cleaning up after any more *goddamned* dogs! That's it!"

I remedied this childhood dog deprivation as a young adult, my wife and I rescuing first three shepherd-mix dogs and learning that I could deal with most low- to moderate-shedding dogs. When it came time to choose a family dog, I wasn't sure which breed would work best. We were a family of four with a three-bedroom, detached Federal, and no one was home during school hours. We were two working parents and two pre-hormonal boys. The ideal candidate would be:

Short-haired;

Low maintenance;

Agreeable, but not overly needy;

Long-lived enough to stick around, God willing, at least until the boys finished high school and, preferably, college;

Small enough to (a) manage, um, input and output efficiently enough to foist that and other chores off on the boys, and (b) be unable to do much physical damage above baseboard level when left alone;

And large enough to fend off childhood diseases and to be willing to stand his/her own ground with the boys, as required.

Those considerations, along with Geri's imprinted girlhood bias, led us to a litter of mini doxie pups who, it was mutually assumed, were somewhere on the other side of the AKC tracks—hence, the asking price and lack of complications. Frank was the only one not fighting, frisking and falling all over his outsize feet in that six-week-old way. He sat apart, motionless, and never took his eyes off us. He embarrassed and intrigued us into taking him home.

Okay...about the name. I was against a precious, cutesy name for a small dog. My solution was a *double entendre,* played off the more familiar "wiener" or "weenie" dog, to wit, "Frank." Geri agreed, but my self-satisfaction was short-lived. Not only did I have to explain its meaning, anyway, but friends familiar with my story would invariably ask, with Oedipal gravity, "Why did you name your dog after your father?"

Frank's childhood was a little rocky, attributably mostly to human error—mine. To train him, I combined two crude concepts, "papers" and "outside," and spread newspapers both on the kitchen floor and outside the entrances. Unable to catch him with an urge, I created "sessions." Reaching what I thought to be a respectable interval, I'd take him outside, place him on the papers and wait expectantly. He'd park himself in the middle of the pulp and give me his most tolerant look, as if to say, "Okay, Chief. What's next?" I would stand there in the cold and wet, knowing my family was watching with amusement through the window.

Eventually it all worked out, but this was a dog

that wanted someone nearby at all times. Dachshunds are renowned for feeling separation anxiety and taking revenge, and if he felt abandoned, he would resort to his untrained puppy ways. We arranged for a pet sitter to look in on him while we went north to Delaware for Christmas break. On our return she sang his praises, took the check and left. It soon became plain that she'd left the door to the basement open, and he'd exploited that loophole; fortunately, the floor was vinyl tile. In the end, he swallowed his pride, to keep the peace, and trained us.

Frank did us the courtesy of respecting Geri and me as the general governing authority, in that order—mostly because she hoisted him onto our bed one night at his first plaintive puppy plea, which he seized upon as a *carte blanche* entitlement. The eventual compromise was between our California king and a folded quilt on the floor nearby, which we called "Flap." He'd ask routinely for the first, but if ordered otherwise, he'd plod glumly away, ears down, as though wading through molasses—followed by a grand and deliberate show of bedding down on the Flap. (Dachshunds are instinctive burrowers, having been bred to hunt badgers, and they like to sleep covered. Before retiring, they find it necessary to fashion a trench in which to recline safely, so they scratch, dig and hump up their spines while imaginary dirt flies out from under their haunches. Robert Benchley observed that "a dog teaches a boy fidelity, perseverance, and to turn around three times before lying down." For pure amusement, then, this was a value-added service.) To this day, when one of us has difficulty getting settled, the other will bark out that command of yore, "Lie down and go to sleep, Frank!"

Befitting his species-neutral given name, Frank established himself quickly with the boys as "the other brother." He was always available to them without condition or stint for real, adolescent play. To be sure, he enjoyed "fetch the ball" in that maddening, "I've got it now. Come get it, sucker!" dachshund way, but right from the start he was always "we," not "they." While he acquiesced to being a love object for us adults and extended family, including my "Auntie Mame" mother-in-law, Ginny, he was all about Trevor and Bevan to the end of his life. In combat, they both did him the favor of shrieking and flopping around on the floor while he vanquished them at the wrist with his mouth.

Frank adapted himself to their disparate personalities. Trevor was his favorite family-room snuggle buddy because, unlike Bevan, he didn't become so absorbed in MTV's *The Real World* that he neglected his petting and treat obligations. Because he was generally more aggressive, Bevan had to be reminded on occasion of his size-ratio boundaries with a growl or nip. When they were out, Frank waited vigilantly at the front window for them to return. The boys took to calling him Ma

Bell because from the shoulders up, with ears elevated, he looked like an antiquated telephone set.

Almost Zen-like in disposition, Frank was made anxious by only three things: going to the vet; fireworks; and water, whatever evil form it took. He handled doctor visits with Gandhi-like civil disobedience, having to be carried and manipulated by hand. We learned to avoid fireworks altogether after taking him with us to watch the legendary National Mall Independence Day celebration from across the Potomac, at the Pentagon, when he was just a year old. He was content in Geri's lap until the first flash bang; then he disappeared—under her blouse. I remember her saying, "I think he's trying to mate with my spine!" From then on, he stayed home. And water? Total freak-out. When the boys were sledding or tubing, he'd run alongside in full cry, biting at the carriage. If the boys were swimming, he'd circle the pool, shrieking and biting the water. The first and only time he encountered the Pacific Ocean, he alternated between running away from the incoming surf and snapping at it on its way back. It was clear to him, and not lost on us, that we were being protected.

Frank never met a guest or a lap he couldn't conquer, without so much as a bark or a whine—in large part because he could stare down the Sphinx without blinking. He'd confront his intended victim and, if not invited aboard immediately, settle in and engage for as long as it took. At their first encounter, my baby sister, Carol, was wary of Frank meeting her husband, Don. She revealed, "He doesn't like whiny, yappy little dogs." It was less than fifteen minutes, door to sofa, before Frank was inside his very happy new friend's shirt.

In short, Frank was not just ours, he was *us,* in whatever incarnation required. He was embarrassed by the whole dog butt-sniffing ritual and considered other canines' loud, energetic curiosity about him undignified. In fact, his only acknowledgment of another's very existence was a cursory woof, uttered after that other creature was safely out of range. For fifteen years, until his brothers had graduated from college and it was the late summer of 2000, he was the perfect relative and ever-accommodating host. Bevan was competing in the Olympic trials, trying to win a spot in the sport he'd excelled in at college—decathlon. Dozens of family and friends passed through our house to offer encouragement. Frank was already in decline, and the sheer numbers of kneecaps and laps simply overwhelmed him.

On the day Geri and I carried him to the vet for his final injection, it was we who were anxious—upset and tearful. We held and caressed him; as he sensed and yielded to the phenobarbital, he regarded us one last time with that calm, transcendent gaze. "Don't grieve for me," he seemed to say. "It was a good run, but it's time for my karma to be reborn."

Good boy, Frank.

Little Orange

Trina Drotar

I first saw the cat one late spring evening, and he seemed to say, "I'm here, and if you can spare a bite to eat, I'd be most appreciative." Of course, he didn't speak those words. In fact, he didn't meow or purr or make any other sound.

When I returned with a bowl of food, he stepped left into the hydrangeas and camellias. I waited for him to approach. He waited for me to leave. I went back inside and peeked at him through the peephole. He sat and ate without greed.

He returned several times, usually in the evening, over the next few weeks, and we formed a sort of dance. He always led. I'd step out, squat and speak to him before extending my hand. He'd take one step back, always remaining just out of arm's reach.

I'd check each evening for Little Orange, calling his

name, even though I wasn't sure that he knew he had a name, much less what it was. I'd walk to the sidewalk, searching for him; I'd sneak peeks through the front door peephole; and I'd even check the backyard. Days passed. I was called out of town for two weeks. The caretaker didn't spot Little Orange.

Days and weeks passed, and then one sunny morning, when I pulled the blinds in the living room, I saw him sunning himself in the backyard. "Little Orange," I yelled. I placed some food and water on the back patio. We danced. We kept that appropriate distance. He spent the better part of the day in the backyard, first in the grass, then under the azaleas near the fence. It was much cooler there, in the dirt, under the shade of the evergreens, the red maple and the Japanese maple. He left sometime before dinner.

I looked daily for him. Scanned both yards, looked up and down the street, called his name. I peered from behind curtains and through the peephole, but there was no sign of Little Orange. That was nearly two months ago.

About two weeks ago, on a Monday morning, when I was headed to the store, I saw an orange/yellow presence on the back patio. I ran to the door. The cat was limping, favoring the left side of his body. He was thin, much thinner than the cat I had danced with. I opened the door and went to him, forgetting that we'd never actually had physical contact. He turned his dirty head and hissed, but he didn't run. I backed up, told him he was safe, and assured him that I'd return with food and water.

He hissed as I placed the bowls on the cement. He hissed again as I backed up. He wobbled to the bowls. He didn't sit to eat, as he'd done before. He stood. I also stood as I watched him eat all the kibble in the dish. I stood as he drank from the water bowl. I wept. Where had he been these past months?

"I need a towel and the cat carrier," I said.

I waited until Little Orange had finished drinking before I approached with the towel. I figured that I'd wrap the towel around him in case he tried to bite or scratch. Just then, another stray entered the yard and a chase ensued. I screamed. I cried. I chased both cats. The other cat had been friendly toward me and had a companion, but I was worried about Little Orange.

Thinking they had both jumped the privacy fence, I ran to the front. One cat. Not Little Orange. I went back through the house to the backyard and spotted him. He ran with all that he had, hobbling and favoring that left side. He leapt at the back fence. I knew we'd lose him if he crossed it. He clung to the top, unable, or as I'd prefer to think, unwilling, to pull his body up and over. I placed the towel around him and brought his toweled body to the house. With my roommate's help, I placed him in the carrier and closed it.

Whatever Little Orange had experienced, I'd never know, but his ordeal increased with the visit to the vet's office where I'd taken my pets for more than two decades.

I'd advised the desk personnel that the cat was feral, that it was injured, and that it was undernourished and probably dehydrated. I gave his name as Little Orange and completed the necessary paperwork before being shown into an exam room. The tech opened the carrier; Little Orange popped his head out, eyes crusted black, burrs on his head; and the tech tipped the carrier. She didn't want to handle this little cat. Still frightened from the earlier chase, Little Orange fell from the exam table before my roommate or I could catch him. The tech simply stood. Little Orange scrambled for the door, hissing.

My roommate picked him up. The tech insisted on taking Little Orange to the back for the exam. We said we'd carry him.

"You're not allowed back there," the tech said.

In hindsight, we should have left then, but we were both exhausted. We allowed the tech to take Little Orange, and then we paced the exam room until the doctor appeared.

"That cat is out of control. He is an unneutered

male, and he scratched me and tried to bite me," she said and continued to call him everything except pure evil.

My roommate and I looked at one another. He'd never been that way, not even when I pulled him from the fence. The hissing, I knew, was his only defense. The doctor suggested this test or that test, but only after we badgered her. Her first suggestion was euthanization. Immediately.

"Can we be there?" I asked.

"Absolutely not," she said, adding that she'd give him a sedative first.

"Absolutely not," we said in unison.

We spent the next thirty minutes phoning a friend who works with feral cats, another who loves cats and yet another who is known for having a solid head. One said that we needed to have the basic tests for HIV and feline leukemia done. Those would inform our next step. The tests came back negative. Good news. One friend then suggested we take the cat to the SPCA for medical care.

The next step was a complete blood panel to rule out kidney and liver disease, which we would have the SPCA do. Another thirty minutes passed before we told the vet that we would take the cat to the SPCA. It took ten minutes for them to retrieve Little Orange.

"He's much calmer," the tech said.

We drove away, intent on going to the SPCA.

Turned out that it was closed on Mondays. We took Little Orange home and quarantined him in the spare bathroom. We put blankets and towels down, a litter box, food and water. He didn't jump out of the carrier, as my other cats always did. He remained there until later that night, when I tipped the carrier. I helped him onto the bed we'd made for him out of towels and blankets. Little Orange was covered with burrs.

We made additional calls that evening, with the intention of bringing him to the SPCA the next morning. One friend suggested we try her vet. I phoned Dr. K's office the next morning. We took Little Orange to the office. He hissed once at Dr. K. After the exam, we asked about blood tests. He ordered the tests. He told us that the cat was very ill. He suggested fluids for Little Orange.

We took Little Orange home, his neck fuller because of the subcutaneous fluids he'd received. He licked my finger clean of the canned food I offered and let me know when he was full. We purchased additional bedding for him.

Partial test results that evening indicated no kidney or liver problems. That, combined with the doctor's proclamation that Little Orange had a strong heart and strong lungs, gave us hope. With fluids, food, rest and safety, he'd grow stronger, like another cat I'd rescued several years earlier.

For the next few days, we changed his bedding at least twice daily, fed him by hand and checked on him. When he refused the cat food, we searched for something different. We brought home baby food instead. Beef and beef gravy had the highest iron count. Dr. K's main concern was Little Orange's anemia. His red blood cells were not being replenished. Dr. K indicated that the anemia went beyond the cat's flea infestation. We purchased flea medicine and applied it to his already ravaged body. Flea dirt, we soon discovered, covered nearly every part of his tiny body. He'd likely been lying in the brush for a long time. There fleas had set up house and multiplied and used the already weak cat for their own nourishment and procreation.

On Wednesday I thought he'd died on the trip from Dr. K's office. Little Orange lived. I moved him onto the bedding when we got home. That was the day I began stroking his body. I'd touched his head a couple of times. He'd flinched. He seemed to enjoy the stroking of his fur. I began, also, to cut away the burrs that had wedged their way into his fur.

Thursday seemed to mark a turning point. He raised his head and turned toward the bathroom door. Three times. The baby food, which he continued to lick from my finger, but only after sniffing it each and every time, and the subcutaneous fluids seemed to be working. We had been prepared to take him to the vet that morning. He wasn't ready.

I spent nearly every day, nearly every waking hour with Little Orange during that week. I brushed his fur with an old soft-bristle pet brush. He purred. I doubted that Little Orange had ever been touched by a human, ever been brushed, ever been held. When I changed his bedding, I held him. I pulled his frail, limp body close to mine so that he might feel my warmth and my heart.

Friday brought another injection of fluids. Dr. K reminded us that the office was open Saturdays in case we needed anything. Although there'd been indications throughout the week that Little Orange was getting stronger, Dr. K told us there might be some brain or spinal cord injury, things only specialists could diagnose. Dr. K never once treated Little Orange as a feral—only as our pet. He suggested a cortisone shot, saying that the shot was usually recommended by specialists.

We returned home, and I spent most of Friday with him, brushing him and trying to feed him, changing his wet bedding, removing burrs from all parts of his body. He needed to retain some of the dignity he had exhibited when he came to us. As much dignity as a cat unable to stand on its own could.

Little Orange, or Orange, as we affectionately called the peaceful orange/yellow tabby, refused to eat late Friday night. That refusal continued through Saturday morning. He refused to drink. He was unable to lift his head, his torso or his limbs. I held him, cried, told him that we loved him. He demanded nothing. He never fought.

We agreed that only Dr. K could tend to Orange. The office was officially closed when we arrived, but Dr. K ushered us in. I cried tears for Little Orange, for the life he had never had the chance to experience, for the love we'd shown him, for the other cats who had entered and left my life, and for me. I wanted to save him, wanted him to grow stronger. After all, he had strong lungs and a strong heart, and his kidneys and liver and pancreas were healthy. Years ago, a doctor told me that I'd know when the end was near.

I held Little Orange in my arms as I carried him to the exam room. Dr. K examined him again, said this was best. My roommate and I stroked Little Orange. He never convulsed.

We wrapped his body, blessed him and placed him in a hole we'd dug in front of the azaleas, under the Japanese maple, shaded by the red maple, near the spot he'd rested two months earlier. We marked the spot with a white fence, autumn leaves and a ceramic garden hummingbird.

The Old Barrel Racer

Elaine Ambrose

By the summer of my twelfth year, my parents had already decided that I was a problem child. There had been too many calls to the school principal's office to discuss my noisy and disruptive behavior in class. (Obviously, they failed to appreciate my spirited, creative nature.) And my teachers had complained that I daydreamed too much. (Couldn't anyone recognize a potential writer here?) And my parents were weary of my fights with my brothers, noting that the boys never questioned the rigid rules of our home. (My brothers later suffered from painful ulcers and other health ailments; however, I did not.)

I grew up on an isolated potato farm near Wendell, Idaho, a nearsighted, left-handed, goofy girl with wrinkly hair and absolutely no ability to conform. Outside of farm chores, the only activity for youth in the farming community of one thousand was a program called 4-H. Desperately hoping it would help me focus, my mother enrolled me in a 4-H cooking class, with the admonition that I behave and not embarrass her. I failed both assignments. When it came my turn to do the demonstration in front of the group, I dropped a dead mouse into the cake batter because I thought it was a brilliant way to spice up the boring meetings. But the leader, one of the town's most prominent women, thought otherwise, and she called my mother and told her I was never welcome in her home again. My mother is still mad at me more than forty years later for the public humiliation.

My great escape from the chores and challenges of life on the farm was to ride my horse, Star. As we galloped through the forty-acre pastures, I hollered with delight when she jumped the ditches and raced to the far end of the field. Sometimes I would lean over, lace my fingers through her long white mane and push my boots against her flanks until she ran full speed, ears back, nostrils flared, with a force of freedom that no bridle could control. When she finally stopped at the top of a hill, her sides were heaving and covered with sweat. Her entire body shivered as she calmed down, and I would jump off and loosen the cinch on the saddle. For me, the exhilaration was worth the fear of falling.

Star was a big white horse, over fourteen hands

high (almost fifty-eight inches from the ground), and had been trained as a prizewinning barrel racer. My father had acquired the horse from a man who owed him money, and the horse was all he had to give. At ten years old, she was past her prime for the rodeo, but I didn't care. She was my passport to liberty, and I loved her.

During the summer of 1964, I worked in the fields during the morning and rode my horse every afternoon. I knew how to catch her in the pasture, bring her to the barn and put on her bridle and saddle. I would be gone all day, and no one ever checked on me. Probably, they were just as eager to have me out of the house as I was to leave. After every ride I brushed Star's hide and fed her oats. Sometimes I brought her an apple or some sugar cubes. My brothers referred to her as an old gray mare, but to me, she was a gorgeous white horse who could run like the wind. And she was my best friend.

One day I learned about a 4-H club for horses. It took expert negotiation skills and outright begging to convince my parents to let me join. "No more dead mice!" I assured them. With the help of the club, I learned how to ride my horse as she raced around three barrels set in a dirt arena. She knew what to do, and all I did was hang on for dear life. She loved the full gallop after rounding the third barrel, and within weeks, we were the fastest team in the club.

"You should ride her at the barrel race at the Gooding County Fair and Rodeo," my 4-H leaders said, encouraging me. "And she should do well, even though she's not so young anymore." Again, I resorted to theatrical pleading to receive my parents' permission. I also needed silver cowboy boots, a purple saddle blanket and a purple vest to ride with the 4-H club. That required extra days of working in the field for one dollar an hour, hoeing beets and weeding potatoes. Soon I had enough money, and I was ready for the fair and rodeo at the end of August.

Two weeks before the fair and rodeo, I used bleach and water in a bucket to comb through Star's long mane and tail to make them gleaming white. Then I saddled her for a solo practice in the pasture. Just as we were riding toward the first barrel, a flock of pheasants suddenly flew up in front of us. Star jumped to the side and I lost my grip. I flew through the air and landed on my right foot. I screamed as it broke.

Star trotted back to me and lowered her head. I couldn't tell her to go get help. My only choice was to get to the three-rail fence and try to climb back on the horse. I grabbed the loose reins and told her to back up. She understood my command and slowly backed to the fence, pulling me through the dirt. We finally reached the fence and I managed to pull myself up on my good foot. Then I climbed up and straddled the top rail.

"Come here, Star," I said. "Easy now." She pressed against the fence so I could fall across the saddle. Then I sat up, secured my left boot in the stirrup and reached for the reins. That was when I noticed her mouth was bleeding, because the bit had rubbed it raw while she was pulling me. That was the only time I cried.

We rode back to the barn and found one of the hired hands, a gnarly old guy named Titus. He helped me off the horse and into his pickup truck. "I'll get you home and then take care of the horse," he said. "And I have some ointment for her mouth." I was grateful.

Going to the doctor was an inconvenience for many farm families. It just wasn't done without considerable effort and a good reason. "Are you sure it hurts?" my father asked. "Maybe it's just sprained?" After much debate, reinforced by my contorted expressions, my mother decided to take me to town to see the doctor. I closed my eyes as they cut off my jeans and sliced through my new silver boot. I heard mumbling as my swollen foot was examined and x-rayed. Then I felt the cold, messy cast being applied to my foot and leg.

"Stay off of it for six weeks," the doctor said, and the words echoed like a prison sentence.

"But I'm competing in the barrel race at the rodeo in two weeks," I said.

My mother and the doctor laughed.

I did not see any humor in the situation. "I'm riding," I said with all the conviction I could muster.

The doctor handed me some crutches and patted my head. "Go home now, dearie, and get some rest," he said. That was when I knew I would ride.

The following day I called Todd Webb, my 4-H leader, and explained the situation. He seemed reluctant to talk with my parents about the barrel-racing competition. "I just need help getting on Star," I said. "She knows what to do. Please let me try."

Todd Webb approached my father that night and, after a few shots of Crown Royal, convinced him that all I had to do was sit on the horse. And basically that was true. Somehow my father agreed, and I was thrilled.

The day before the race, Todd Webb and several 4-H club members came around with horse trailers to get the horses. By then, I was using only one crutch and could maneuver quite well with my clunky cast. We drove to the stables at the fair grounds and unloaded the horses, our gear and extra bales of hay. Star seemed nervous, so I brushed her hide and sang my favorite song from our lazy riding days—"We'll Sing in the Sunshine," by Gale Garnett. The song had the perfect cadence for an afternoon ride.

The next day we all arrived early to prepare for the race. The right leg of my jeans was split to cover the cast. The club members assisted in hoisting the saddle onto Star, joking that I would need to split any prize money with them. Star's mouth had healed, but I decided to pull a hackamore without a bit over her head. I struggled onto the horse and took the reins. I felt comfortable, except the cast caused my leg to stick straight out, and I knew it would hit the first barrel as Star galloped around it.

"Tie me down," I said to Todd Webb. He hesitated but then agreed. He used a small rope to secure my right leg to the stirrup.

"Don't fall," he said. "Or we're both in trouble."

We trotted to the arena and joined the other riders. I supported my weight on my thighs and left boot as we rode in a slow lope around the arena. I could feel Star getting tense. She had owned this competition many years ago, and I knew she was eager to return. "Easy, Star," I murmured. "We can do it."

There were seven riders ahead of us in the race, and we were last. They all posted times between twenty and fifteen seconds. Star's ears were rigid as we eased into the chute. I matched her breathing as we waited for the countdown. Suddenly the gate flew open and Star shot out in a fury of speed. She leaned around the first barrel and my cast rubbed the side. Then she ran toward the second barrel and circled it so sharply that I could touch the ground. Then she sped toward the third barrel. We rounded it and headed toward home. Dirt flew, the crowd cheered and my cast banged against the rope as I rode the relentless force of pure energy. I knew my magnificent horse was running to win. We crossed the finish line in fourteen seconds and the crowd went wild. The clumsy problem child and the old horse were the improbable winners.

I don't remember all the details after that. I know I looked into the stands and saw my parents and brothers and couldn't believe they were cheering for me. The five-hundred-dollar prize money, a fortune back then, was added to my college savings account. Star and I never raced again. After that day she became slower and less eager to run free. We still took regular rides, and she would pick up the pace as I sang. But we had nothing else to prove.

My foot healed, I entered high school and I didn't have much time to ride. Star spent her last days roaming the fields, and every now and then she would raise her head, point her ears and break into a full gallop. The last time I saw her, she was jumping a ditch on the far side of the pasture. She died while I was away at college, and my mother called and asked if I wanted to see her before they took her away. "No," I answered. "She'll always be alive for me. Every time I need to get around an obstacle, I'll feel her power." And that's how it remains for me, the wild child who finally grew up with the help of an aging horse and a pounding passion for freedom.

The Dog Who Wouldn't Bark

Meera Klein

The black-and-white photo was old and yellowing, but I could clearly make out the proud stance of the dog and his mistress. I could barely make out the words penciled on the back of the fading photograph: "Leela and Chuppa, 1951." My mother and her beloved dog.

The cool mist swirled around Leela and smothered her in its wet embrace. She shivered and wrapped the woolen shawl more tightly around her slender body. The late November days in Kotagiri were chilly and dismal, nothing like the warm tropical nights she was used to. Leela's sigh sounded loud in the gray silence as she paused to take a deep whiff of the fading jasmine blooms on the vine by the front gate. It was then she heard the sound, the tiniest whimper, which she would have missed if the world hadn't been so silent. She reached up and unlatched the metal gate and stepped onto the patch of grass. In the dim twilight she could make out a small bundle lying on the wilted jacaranda blooms. When she looked closely, she saw it was a tiny shivering puppy. She couldn't bear to leave it there on the side of the road. She relatched the gate and walked into the kitchen using the side entrance.

The kitchen was warm and cozy. Her mother, Ammalu, was seated on a small wooden stool in front of the hearth, stirring a pot of lentil stew. The sharp scent of cumin mingled with the wet puppy smell. Ammalu wrinkled her nose.

"What do you have there?" she asked, getting up to take a closer look at the black-and-tan bundle in Leela's arms.

"Oh, Amma," Leela wailed. "Look what someone dropped off at our front gate."

The puppy seemed to know it was being inspected and opened its tiny jaws and yawned, stretching out a minuscule pink tongue.

"Not everyone has your kind heart, my daughter," Ammalu sighed. "Remember what our neighbor Sister Mary told us?"

Leela nodded and held the puppy closer to her chest. Their nearest neighbor, an Anglo-Indian everyone called Sister Mary, lived a few miles down the road and was a feisty animal lover.

"Be warned. Villagers get rid of their unwanted pets by dropping them off at the bungalows in the middle of the night. Most of us are only too happy to take in these dogs and cats. It's a shame, though, because not everyone wants a stray and that is the end of the poor animal," she'd lamented.

That will not happen to this little one, Leela silently vowed. Mother and daughter dried the puppy and fed the hungry creature some rice gruel. Soon the little dog was curled up on a pile of rags in front of the warm hearth.

The next morning Ammalu mixed a little rice and vegetable broth in a beautiful ceramic pan decorated with deep purple flowers and urged the little puppy to eat out of the fancy bowl.

"Amma, why are you using such a nice dish for the dog?" Leela protested.

"Leela, you know I don't like to use these tainted containers."

The tainted containers Ammalu was referring to were part of a collection of dinnerware left behind by the previous owner. After the declaration of independence in 1947, many British decided to leave India rather than live in a country no longer ruled by Great Britain. Rather than pack up an entire household, some of them left many things behind. One such Englishman was the owner of the charming bungalow that was now Leela's home on the outskirts of the remote hill station town of Kotagiri, nestled among the famous Blue Mountains, or Nilgiris.

When they moved into the charming red-tiled house in late 1948, they found the musty rooms filled with large pieces of wooden furniture. The cabinet doors were inlaid with ceramic tile in beautiful geometric patterns. An intricate carved folding screen in one of the three bedrooms provided privacy and beauty. The dining room boasted a large china buffet, complete with silver soup tureens, round and oval serving platters, big serving bowls and a tea set. The delicate moss-green tea set, made of the finest bone china, would never be used, though. Like most upper-caste Indians, Ammalu's family was vegetarian. They had no intention of eating or drinking from vessels used by strangers and nonvegetarians. At the first opportunity Ammalu invited friends, neighbors and acquaintances from the surrounding areas to come choose from the lovely Spode plates and Wedgwood dinnerware. So the puppy happily ate off the Spode chinaware and drank from his Wedgwood saucer.

The German shepherd turned out to be the most patient of animals. He waited for Leela or Ammalu to get up each morning and let him out. He would wander around the front yard, sniffing at rosebushes and lifting his leg against the spindly poinsettia tree. He would then lie on the kitchen floor, his bright blue eyes following Leela's every movement.

"He really is the most silent dog," a friend remarked to Leela. That was when she came up with the perfect name for her new pet, Chuppa, or "the silent one."

She tried out the new name, calling, "Chuppa!" Immediately the puppy sat up, straight and proud. He cocked his head and looked at Leela as if waiting for a command. From then on Leela spent countless hours with the young dog, teaching him simple commands. Chuppa was an intelligent pup and wanted to please Leela. He became the young girl's constant companion. He would greet her joyously, albeit silently, every afternoon when she returned from school. He draped his long tan-and-black body across Leela's doorway. The pair was a common sight as they went on long walks among the tea bushes and apple and pear orchards.

One evening, when Ammalu made a teasing gesture toward Leela, pretending to hit her, Chuppa immediately sat up and stared at Ammalu and emitted a soft warning growl.

"Chuppa thinks I was going to hit you!" Ammalu exclaimed. "What a good dog. Don't worry, Chuppa, I would never hit my girl." Ammalu bent down and petted the agitated pup, who settled down, his head resting on his folded paws, as if he understood Ammalu's words.

Leela decided to teach the dog commands to make sure he would know when a threat was real and when a family member was just playing. The dog took to the lessons as if he was a sponge soaking up spilled water.

Two years later Chuppa was a full-grown German shepherd with thick black-and-tan fur and bright blue eyes. He was a familiar sight in the little village and allowed young children to pet and fuss over him. But his soft eyes were always on Leela.

A few months later, their postman, the deliverer of news and mail, had some disturbing gossip. "Did you hear about the thefts?" he asked Ammalu and Leela one afternoon. "There has been a rash of thefts in the area and residents are asked to keep their gates locked."

The following spring Ammalu and Unny, Leela's older brother, had to make one final trip to their ancestral village to take care of some business, and Ammalu was not happy to leave Leela.

"Don't worry, Amma. Chuppa will keep me company at night, and during the day Mala and her husband will be here," Leela assured her mother.

Mala and Lingam were local villagers who came to help Leela's family with household chores. Ammalu and Unny were expected to be gone for about five days, and after giving Mala and Lingam many instructions about the household and Leela's personal safety, they finally left.

That evening Leela made sure all the doors were locked before retiring to the living room. A fire in the hearth made the room snug and comfortable. Chuppa settled down in front of the fire and Leela curled up on the sofa with a Sherlock Holmes mystery.

"Why didn't the dog bark?" she murmured to herself.

Chuppa glanced up with a questioning look in his blue eyes.

"Don't mind me, Chuppa. I'm just talking about the clue in this story," she assured her pet, who sighed and went back to staring at the golden flames.

The crackling fire was the only sound in the room and Leela found herself drifting off. Chuppa's low growl woke her up.

"Shh…Chuppa. It's just the fire."

But the dog didn't settle down; instead he stood up and looked toward the front hallway. The coarse hairs on his neck were standing up and his body was tense and alert. Leela was alarmed at the dog's stance and got up to stand in the living room doorway. She was as tense as Chuppa and tried to hear what had disturbed the dog.

Then she heard it, the slightest grating of metal as

the front gate was opened. Chuppa growled beside her. She put a hand on his head, wondering what to do.

"Is anyone home?" a woman's voice called out from the front stoop. Leela knew whoever was out there had probably seen the warm glow of the light through the living room window, even though the cloth curtains were drawn shut.

Leela took a deep breath and walked into the dark hallway. She turned on the porch light and lifted up the curtain to peer through the front window. She could make out the figure of a woman and a man standing on the front porch steps. The woman raised a slim hand and knocked on the wooden door. Leela looked back at Chuppa and gestured for him to stand behind her. The dog obediently went into the hallway, where he was hidden in the shadows behind his mistress.

Even though she dreaded opening the door, Leela decided it was better than waiting for the couple to perhaps break the glass and force their way in. She pulled the door open and peered out.

"Who are you, and why are you knocking on my door at this time of the night?"

The woman laughed, a sound that was nervous and at the same time somehow threatening. "Sister, we are just poor pilgrims on our way to the temple on the hill. Can you spare us a hot drink or a few paise?"

"I'm sorry, but my hearth is out for the night and I

have no change. Perhaps you can find hospitality farther down the road," Leela said.

"Listen here, sister," the man snarled, pushing the woman aside. "We are not asking for a few paise like beggars. We are demanding you hand over your necklace, earrings and anything else of value you have in the house. I don't make idle threats." As he spoke, he pulled out a knife, the blade glinting in the overhead porch light.

"I don't like threats. I suggest you leave," Leela said, trying not to sound as frightened as she felt.

The man answered by pushing the door aside and taking a step to come inside. A deep rumble from the hallway stopped him in mid-stride.

"Chuppa, come here," Leela called out to her faithful companion, who came to stand beside her. He bared his teeth and he gave out a menacing growl. The couple stared at the German shepherd.

"Now, I suggest you leave before my dog gets impatient," Leela said to the couple.

The man hissed in anger. "A dumb animal isn't going to stop me," he said in a low tone as he stepped toward Leela, his knife raised.

"Chuppa, get the knife," Leela ordered in a firm voice.

Without a moment's hesitation, the dog leaped and grabbed the man's hand. The knife clattered to the ground. The man yelped in surprise. Leela quickly kicked the knife out of his reach. The dog let go of the man's hand and waited for his next command.

"Good dog. Now get him," Leela said.

Again the dog leaped and, using his full weight, brought the man down. Chuppa placed a heavy paw on the man's chest and bared his teeth. The woman cried out, and the dog looked at her with his soft eyes and pulled back his lips to show his sharp white teeth.

"Call off your dog," the woman cried. "We meant no harm."

The silence was broken by a murmur of voices.

"Miss Leela, are you all right?" a voice asked from the driveway. It was Lingam. He was carrying a smoky homemade torch in his hand. Behind him there were several villagers.

"Lingam! I am so glad to see you," Leela called and sighed in relief. "Chuppa has caught a man who was threatening me."

Lingam walked up to the porch steps and looked down at the figure on the ground.

"These look like the couple who have been robbing houses," he announced. "We heard they were out tonight, and came by to check on you. But it looks like you can take care of yourself." His white teeth flashed as he grinned at Leela.

"It was Chuppa who saved the day," Leela said. "Chuppa, let him go."

The German shepherd looked down at the man and growled again before moving slowly off him. The animal went to stand beside Leela, looking up at her with adoration shining from his bright blue eyes.

Leela bent down and hugged the dog. She buried her face in his doggy fur. "Thank you, Chuppa," she whispered.

"Woof." Chuppa's bark was short and soft. Leela laughed out loud. That was the one and only time Chuppa ever barked.

For years the dog was my mother's faithful companion in Kotagiri. When he died of old age, my mother was heartbroken. Chuppa was the last pet she ever owned.

In Touch with One's Felines

Ed Goldman

The crying starts as soon as the car starts. "It'll be all right," I say as softly as I can, while still fighting to be heard. "Daddy loves you," I add, figuring there may be some doubt on her part.

I'm already soaked with perspiration by the time I reach the end of the block, the crying now reaching such a feverish, intense pitch that I debate pulling over and reprimanding her. But how can I? She won't understand and won't care that this is proving more traumatic for me than it ever will be for her. So I take a deep breath, crank up Mozart's Turkish March on the classical station and keep telling myself, *The hospital is only a mile and a half away....*

Every three days I take my wife's seventeen-year-old cat, Sabrina, to the Sacramento Animal Hospital for intravenous fluid treatments. They slow down her metabolism, and that keeps her from burning too many calories too fast. Early in her treatments, she weighed four pounds and eleven ounces. Now she's up to six pounds and two to four ounces, depending on how much of her dinner and then our dinner she eats the night before.

I inherited Sabrina when my wife, Candy, and I began our life together four years ago. The little cat is beautiful and calls to mind a black-and-white Puss in Boots. She also has lungs that would prompt even an opera conductor to say, "Easy." When I drive her to the treatments, she howls from the moment I strap her carrier into the backseat until the moment when I get her home, unstrap the carrier and let her strut back up the stairs to the house, as though she went to the vet only because she felt like it.

Sometimes between the hours of 4:00 and 6:00 a.m., she yowls, which is worse than howling, from the first floor of our three-story home. It's a home with a contemporary, open floor plan. This means the only sound barriers are the earplugs I keep on a shelf behind my pillow.

I'd never had a cat before, only a couple of dogs. My first dog was a rescue dog, in the truest sense of the word. One evening my first wife (bear with me, as there are a total of three) and I were riding back from dinner with another couple in Long Beach, California. As we came to a stoplight, I noticed there was a very panicked mutt on the island separating the opposing lanes of traffic. She was panting heavily, and that was her only activity since she was, literally, paralyzed with fear. Since my wife and I were passengers, I asked my friend not to go when the light changed (we made many friends that evening). I jumped out of the car, hunched down on the island, about twenty feet from the little dog, and put my arms out. "Come on," I said as softly as I could above the din of traffic, the shouted assertions about my parentage (our *many* friends), the cursing and the honking from the cars behind us.

Miraculously, the dog dashed into my embrace. I all but tossed her into the backseat with my wife and jumped in the car with an athletic grace that surprised everyone in the car, including the dog and me. My friend gunned the car through the intersection just before the light turned red.

Back in our one-bedroom apartment, a block from the ocean, we let the little dog smell her way around before she settled in for the night on the bathroom floor. This turned out to be a measure of her intelligence, because sometime later she experienced an attack of diarrhea, which she thoughtfully dealt with by quickly climbing into the bathtub.

As the days went by, we advertised in the local newspaper that we'd found her (she had no ID tag and this was many years before the invention of the puppy microchip). We hesitantly named the dog Portia—my wife loved Shakespeare—in the hope that we would keep her.

No one answered the ad after a tense ten days. By then, we had taken Portia to the vet (she was fine), had caught her up on her shots (as best as the vet could determine) and had plied our landlady with champagne, chocolates and a hefty damage deposit for allowing us to violate the apartment building's no-pets-or-surfers edict (the latter was implicit; the former clearly spelled out in our lease).

As the years went by, we fell in love with Portia, moved to Sacramento and promptly fell out of love with each other. I adored the dog but knew it would shatter my soon-to-be ex-wife even more than the divorce would if she also had to surrender our dog to me. So when she asked if she could keep Portia, I said, "Of course." Part of me wanted to push for visitation, but I realized that as much as I would miss my dog, in the long term she'd be far better off with my ex-wife.

My second dog was a rescue dog, too, from the SPCA. I was married to Jane, my second wife, whom I would live with for twenty-nine years, until her death. We got the dog when our daughter, Jessica, was three and a half years old. Jane had always been afraid to have a dog because she suffered from allergies that could easily escalate into asthma. But since our daughter loved animals so much and clearly had a gift for communicating with them—she surreptitiously petted the kangaroos at the San Francisco Zoo, which was strictly *verboten*—Jane asked her allergist what sort of dog she could have that would cause her the least discomfort. "Get whatever you like and we'll adjust your shots," he said.

This came as a shock to her. All her life she'd been told—by uninformed family doctors and a mother who would say, "Who needs the trouble?"—that a dog, *any* dog, unless it was completely shaved and drenched in aloe, would cause her grief. "I'd have had dogs all my life," she said.

Camellia, a German shepherd–Queensland herder admixture, was just eight weeks old when we adopted her. She and our daughter quickly became quibbling siblings, to the extent that when we were enrolling Jessica in a private school and she was asked if she had sisters or brothers, she responded, "I have one sister an' she's a doggy."

Camellia lived with us until she was fourteen (and my daughter was seventeen) and contracted cancer. By this time, my wife was also five years into her nine-year battle with breast cancer. Camellia's losing battle became far too emblematic of the direction our lives would take in the next couple of years: my wife's condition would turn terminal, our daughter would leave home for college, and I would have to learn, or to pretend, that everything in life had a purpose.

I could never stand cats. Part of my animus derived from the fact that I'd always been allergic to them. Another part sprang from the fact that cats just didn't seem needy, dependent, grateful and sloppy enough to make them loving pets. Cats just never seem to need anyone's help. Fact is, I like to be depended on, I like to protect and I like to help. I have the same problem with children once they're old enough to ask you to leave their rooms.

And while I lived with Sabrina and tolerated her, I never really saw myself as a cat owner—not in the way I'd been a dog owner to Portia and Camellia. Until one day, not long ago, a feral neighborhood cat strolled into our backyard and began to hassle Sabrina. She quickly burst into an aria that had me running downstairs from my office into the backyard and removing the intruder, which I threw for a thirty-yard incomplete pass (unless you consider a camellia bush a receiver).

Wow. Where did that come from? I wondered, standing on the grass, waiting for my heartbeat to calm down. My rage and violent reaction surprised me. Since when was I patrolling the garden to protect a cat? I knew enough about cats by then not to await a thank-you note from Sabrina or even a casual brush against my leg as she stalked stiffly back into the house. *Weird,* I thought, shaking my head and brushing the stray cat hairs off my hands. *Just weird.*

A few nights later Jessica came to dinner and asked for my help with a project with a looming due date. The request was barely out of her mouth before I nodded in agreement. "Sure, of course. Let's get started. I'm ready right now."

And that was when I realized why I'd come to Sabrina's rescue. One of my kids had been in trouble. I'd done what any loving father—or cat owner—would do.

Kissing the Whale

Pam Giarrizzo

Laguna San Ignacio is not a destination people generally think about when planning a vacation to Mexico; indeed, most people have probably never even heard of it. It lies on the Pacific Ocean side of Baja California Sur, but visitors don't go there to swim or scuba dive or lie on the beach. Flying into the desert near the lagoon in an airplane so tiny they can't even stand up straight in it, they may start to question why they decided to go there at all. But they are there because they have heard about the *laguna de ballenas amistosas* (lagoon of friendly whales) and they want to see if the stories are really true.

Two years ago I was one of those people, although I wasn't actually the person who was supposed to be there. My husband, Phil, was, since he had been part of a successful campaign a few years earlier to prevent

Mitsubishi Corporation from building a salt plant at the lagoon, which serves as the nursing grounds of the California gray whale. He had been asked by others who had been a part of the campaign to go with them and see the whales for himself. After all the arrangements had been made, pressing business matters arose that kept Phil from taking the trip, and he asked if I would like to go in his stead.

I had gone whale watching before, crowded with strangers along the rail of a large tour boat off the coast of Monterey, fighting seasickness and straining for a glimpse of a whale a quarter of a mile in the distance. I had no desire to take a trip like that again. But I knew that this was not going to be that kind of whale watching. My husband had been told stories about camping out on the beach in Mexico, close enough to hear the whales breathe in the stillness of the night. That sounded like a once-in-a-lifetime whale-watching excursion, and I was grateful for the opportunity.

I packed my gear and flew to San Diego, the jumping-off point for the trip. The chartered bus ride with my fellow whale watchers from San Diego to a small private airport across the border in Tijuana was uneventful. When I saw the small planes we were about to board, I suddenly understood why I had to list my weight on the trip application and was instructed to bring no more than thirty pounds of luggage. It looked like only a dozen or so passengers would fit inside each plane. I found myself worrying about whether or not I had been entirely truthful when I listed my weight, and whether I might have packed a few more things than I really needed.

With a certain amount of trepidation, I climbed the steps to the plane's entrance, hunched forward and squeezed through the narrow passage that served as an aisle, dropping into the first open seat I saw. The lavatory was separated from the cabin by only a flimsy curtain. After takeoff, the person sitting in the last seat in the plane began serving the in-flight meal by reaching into the cooler supplied by the tour operator and passing snacks and soft drinks forward until everyone, including the pilot and copilot, had something to eat. I was beginning to wonder what I had gotten myself into.

Fortunately, the plane touched down without incident on a dusty airstrip in the desert, where we were met by vans and driven several miles to the water's edge. We grabbed our luggage and boarded pangas, small fishing boats about twenty-two feet in length, which delivered us about forty-five minutes later to the Rocky Point campground at Laguna San Ignacio. We unloaded the boats bucket-brigade style, found our assigned cabin tents and received a brief orientation about the camp.

After a quick lunch we headed down to the water and climbed back into the pangas for our first ride out to see the whales. In addition to the pangateers who piloted the boats, there was a naturalist aboard each boat to point out the birds—black-and-white surf scoters, with their striking orange bills; parasitic jaegers, conducting midair attacks to steal fish from the mouths of hapless gulls; and other denizens of the lagoon, such as sea turtles, moving effortlessly through the water. Whales could be seen in the distance, breaching most of their bodies' length out of the water's calm surface or spy hopping just enough to see who was in the vicinity. Bottlenose dolphins appeared from nowhere, bow riding in the surf stirred up by the pangas, much to the delight of all the passengers aboard.

Suddenly, the pangateer cut the throttle, slowing the boat to a quiet glide along the shimmering water. He and the naturalist were especially alert then. The whales that had seemed so distant a moment ago were now a mere fifty feet away. We all held our breath; this was what we'd been waiting for. Slowly, an enormous barnacle-covered gray whale mother made her way toward the panga, which was about half her length. She was followed by her shiny black calf, which, even though it was only a few months old, was already as long as the boat. The whales were only a few feet away, and we were at their mercy, hoping that the stories we'd been told about the friendly whales of Laguna San Ignacio were true, and that they wouldn't upend our panga and spill us into the frigid waters of the lagoon.

"Lean over the side and splash a little water toward them with your fingertips if you want them to come closer," the naturalist advised. There was no question that we wanted the whales to come closer. This was the moment we had dreamed of. The mother whale appeared to show her infant what to do next. She eased closer and closer to the boat, until her head rose up out of the water mere inches from the side of the panga. As she met our gaze, we reached out eagerly and began to stroke her scarred gray head, whispering soothing words to let her know that we, too, were friendly. The encounter continued for a minute or so, before she dived down and resurfaced several feet away on the other side of the boat.

Her calf, who was learning this behavior from his mother, inched closer to the boat, much to our delight, as we couldn't wait to stroke his smooth black head. His body had not yet been invaded by the barnacles and sea lice that had attached themselves to his mother's skin, nor had he suffered the injuries from run-ins with ships or other creatures that had left his mother with deep scars. We continued to pat every part of him that we could reach until his mother finally swam away and he followed after her. We had all heard about people who had managed to actually kiss a whale or rub the baleen plates in its mouth, which are used to filter its food, but for us on our first day in the lagoon, it was enough just to be able to touch the whales. It is not an overstatement to say that this demonstration of trust from creatures who have suffered so much over the centuries at the hands of whalers and other humans was a life-changing experience for me and all the other passengers aboard the tiny fishing boat.

The gray whales of Laguna San Ignacio were not always friendly. They could not afford to be. After the captains of European whaling ships discovered what a fertile hunting area these nursing grounds were, the waters of the lagoon ran red with the blood of slaughtered whales. Then the mother gray whales would attack the whaling ships ferociously in a futile attempt to save themselves and their calves. The whalers called them "hardheaded devil fish" and learned to fear them, even as they harpooned them by the hundreds, hunting them almost to extinction. Not until 1949 did the International Whaling Commission end this bloody practice, once again allowing mother gray whales to give birth to their calves in the peaceful sanctuary of the lagoon and to prepare them for the long migration north to the Bering Sea and beyond.

For decades after the hunting ended, gray whales and local fishermen maintained an uneasy truce, staying as far away from each other as possible. The story of how that all changed is legendary in Laguna San Ignacio. One day in 1972 two local fishermen were out in their panga when they saw a female gray whale heading for them. They tried to get away, but the whale kept coming closer, going so far as to swim under the boat at one point and actually lift it out of the water. After she lowered the boat, she continued to swim near it, making eye contact with the fishermen until one of them finally reached out his hand and touched her. This was the beginning of a new era in the relationship between humans and whales in Laguna San Ignacio. News of the friendly whales began to spread, and people began to arrive from locations near and far to enjoy this mystical experience for themselves. Now tourism has joined fishing as an important source of income for the people who live near the lagoon, and they have become very protective of their whales.

Over dinner in the evenings we learned about the gray whales and the lagoon from the naturalists who had been hired for the season. I had the impression that everyone who made the journey to Laguna San Ignacio must be deeply touched by the experience. It seemed to me that no one who had stroked the head of a baby gray whale would ever see a Save the Whales bumper sticker in the same light again. It would no longer be just a slogan; it would become a sacred trust.

But after a few trips out onto the lagoon, I began to

worry that I might be part of the problem. "Should we be encouraging them like this?" I asked Kate, the naturalist who accompanied the panga I was in one afternoon. "Should we make the whales believe that people are their friends, when on so many levels we are not? Will my loving caresses somehow take away the baby whale's ability to recognize danger if she comes across a whaling ship during her northward migration?" Kate agreed that normally this would be cause for concern, but she assured me that the gray whales exhibited this behavior only in Laguna San Ignacio, where, thankfully, they are protected by laws and local sentiment.

I allowed her words to soothe my newly troubled conscience, but I continued to wrestle with the question of whether we are wrong to allow the whales to become so comfortable with us. After all, one of the cardinal rules of wildlife rehabilitation is to refrain from trying to turn a wild animal into a pet, which means that contact with humans is kept at a minimum. The whales have no need for rehabilitation, as they are already in the wild, but it seems as though the same principle would apply.

Part of my dilemma is that I don't know what's in it for the whales. They approached us, after all. We didn't approach them. The fishermen in 1972 were trying to get away from the whale, but she persisted in forcing their acquaintance. When my fellow whale watchers and I went out into the lagoon, the pangateer didn't chase after the whales. He waited for them to come to us. The whales aren't looking for food, since food is not the primary reason they stay so long in Laguna San Ignacio, and no food is given to them by anyone in the pangas. There are those who believe that the whales seek interaction with humans in order to form a close bond and thereby ensure that we won't threaten to harm them or their calves again. But I know of no research that would support this anthropomorphic theory.

Maybe I'm overthinking this. Maybe I should just trust the whales. If they perceive that there is value in making overtures to humans, who am I to say there is not? Still, I worry.

In our two trips a day out into the lagoon, I don't think we ever went without a visit from a whale, although the tour operators always caution that there is no guarantee of whale encounters. We all became quite adept at coaxing the whales to the side of the panga so we could pat them, but I had an unfulfilled desire to kiss a whale before my trip ended. That seemed a little more difficult, though. Reaching my arm far enough over the side of the small boat to touch a whale with my hand was one thing, but leaning my whole upper body far enough out to kiss the whale was another matter entirely.

On the last day of my trip, I watched for my chance.

I would have loved to kiss a mother whale, if for no other reason than to thank her for trusting us with her calf, but it seemed to me that the mothers always hung back just a bit, making us work a little harder to reach out and touch them. The calves, with their exuberance of youth, were more likely to come closer. With a heightened sense of awareness, I watched as a gray whale calf swam toward the panga. I began to ease up off of my seat and reach out into the water. I splashed a little water in the whale's direction, leaning a little farther out of the boat the closer he came.

Suddenly he was rubbing up against the side of the panga, and everyone was stroking his satiny skin. It was now or never, I thought, and I leaned as far out as I safely could and kissed the side of his head. And then, with salt water still clinging to my lips, I gave him another kiss for good measure. Afterward, I alternated between a feeling of almost giddy excitement and an overwhelming desire to burst into tears. It was an intensely emotional experience, one that I would never have thought possible just weeks earlier.

I had to be in Monterey on business several months ago and I had a little time to kill before my meeting started. I took a walk along Fisherman's Wharf and saw people waiting to go out on a whale-watching cruise. It seemed to me to be awfully late in the season for that, so I stopped and took a look at the trip board set up by one of the cruise operators to find out what they expected to see. It announced recent sightings: Killer whales! Blue whales! Gray whales! And I found myself wondering if any of *my* gray whales were off the coast of Monterey now. Would anyone on that whale-watching cruise, fighting nausea and being jostled by other passengers, see my whales? Would they see the mother whale to whom I felt such gratitude for trusting me with her calf? Would they see the baby whale that I kissed? Probably not, and even if they did see those gray whales, they couldn't possibly feel the same bond to them that I now feel.

Perhaps reasonable minds can differ as to whether it's a good thing or not for people to have such close encounters with whales as I did in Laguna San Ignacio, but one thing is certain: having kissed a baby gray whale, I will always feel that the responsibility for his fate and the fate of his species is in my hands.

In the Nick of Time

Sue Pearson

Family and friends each wrote goodbye notes and put them inside a grave marker, a memorial box that read Beloved Friend. One handwritten note read, "We will love you and miss you forever." My granddaughter's note read, "We will never forget what you did for so many, especially me. Thank you." I tucked in a faded piece of newsprint, a story from almost a dozen years before. The first line read: "When life is moving very fast but everything seems to be in slow motion, you can be sure nothing good is happening. The events speed up the action. The fear slows it down."

Holding the delicate newsprint in my hand, I could still see it all so clearly—Nick was still a puppy then, really—a Lab not yet two years old. Adam was the twelve-year-old friend of my son, Evan. What began as an adventure on a mountain river on a bright, warm, sunny June day was to take a sudden dark turn. It was the day before the first day of summer and the river beckoned. I told the boys they could only go wading and only in one shallow section of the river, upstream, and only if I went with them. It was that compelling an idea to them, even if Mom had to come along, so off we all went, including Nick the dog, to sample the first of summer's refreshments. We arrived at the spot I had dubbed "safe" and the boys proceeded to roll up the legs of their jeans. Nick splashed along the shore, enjoying the cold water rushing by but in no hurry to join the strong currents bent on finding a more tranquil home in the valley. I had taken Nick's leash off to let him play and I stood on the shore, watching the boys and the dog.

Life couldn't be better. Everyone was having one of those moments of simple pleasure that we look back on years later and realize was in fact a treasured memory…one of the reasons life is so sweet. The next moment Adam was joking with Evan…giving him a twelve-year-old's challenge. "Go all the way under, Evan. I dare you!" Evan was laughing and hesitating. Suddenly it was Adam who was all the way under. He'd slipped on the rocks. He was immediately swept into the unforgiving current. In those split seconds, which have now become vivid snapshots of terror engraved in those parts of my brain reserved for life-and-death reactions,

I remember thinking I was watching a tragedy unfold. I ran to the edge of the water and yelled for Adam to catch the dog leash I was about to throw. I missed. He missed. He went under water again, surfaced and looked up at me. His eyes, wild with fear, seemed to plead, "Help me!"

I saw paramedics arrive after Evan ran back to the cabin to get help from his dad. I saw them pull Adam's lifeless body from the chilly water and work on him for an hour. I saw Evan sobbing on the shore, forever changed. I called Adam's parents. There would be no birthday party next Saturday. Instead a funeral. I could never forgive myself for letting the boys go in the water. Adam's loss would weigh us all down for the rest of our lives. None of us would love the little cabin in the mountains again. This landscape would be a tangle of pain and grief and sorrow.

But none of this happened. In those split seconds of heightened awareness I saw a blur of yellow fur flash by. It was Nick. He jumped in the water and swam to Adam as the current thrust the boy away. I saw Adam grab a handful of fur and skin like his life depended on it. It did. Nick never hesitated. He swam to shore, pulling Adam with him. Adam climbed out of the water, shaken and shouting at the same time, "Nick, I love you!" Nick shook himself off and casually walked over to me and sat down.

Thank you, God. And thank you, Nick—for saving us in the nick of time from a lifetime of grief, deep sorrow and regret.

My hero dog, Nick, lived to be thirteen, and not only was his a good life in the country, with ten acres to explore and rule, but it was a life full of more heroic deeds. He had that courage in his DNA. In the years after he saved Adam's life, he was always on duty to perform more acts of courage on behalf of everyone nearby, casually nudging a toddler out of harm's way near a bucking horse, defending a neighbor against an attack by another dog, helping my granddaughter overcome a fear of dogs. He was most dramatically protective of me. When a visiting dog rushed me at full speed, catching me behind the knees to flip me into the air, Nick was there. I landed on a hard slate patio…heard something snap…my femur. The dog was on top of me instantly, mauling me. A snarling Nick with his hackles up bit the dog, pushed the dog away and then kept it at bay until help arrived.

As we closed the memorial box with our notes, which we'd tucked into a plastic bag to keep time and weather from destroying our tributes, we held hands and prayed at Nick's final resting place in a sunny spot on my ranch. "We thank you for this guardian angel who saved lives, chased danger into retreat and washed away fear."

Standing there in the sunlight now, I try to imagine what heaven is like for dogs. I know one exists, because God wouldn't let these loyal creatures go with no reward. It must be a place with not just ten acres, but a million acres, with an eternity of holes to dig and smells to sniff. If it turns out there really are pearly gates to heaven, I see Nick waiting there for me, leash in his mouth, looking forward to another long walk.

Wednesday in the Wall

Chris Fowler (Roller Derby name: Cherry Madness)

The softness of the kitten was a relief in my hands. Her small black form had been wedged in the confines of the brick wall. Now she was safe with me.

It was a Wednesday, a chilly October afternoon, as I worked quickly to unload supplies in a pre-WWII warehouse in downtown Sacramento. This cold warehouse with redbrick and lead-lined walls is the proud home of my team, the Sacred City Derby Girls, a women's flat-track Roller Derby league. It is said to have originally been a WWII ammunition storage facility, then a candy factory sometime in the sixties. Its history is then lost for a few decades. After several years of neglect it was home to a "bounce house turned rave nightclub" venue. We acquired it at an auto auction a few years ago and now had a training ground for a team exuding feminine strength and endurance, a team of derby girls. On this blustery fall day, three members of Sacred City were brought to a stiff standstill with the softest "meew" from inside the walls.

"Stop!" I suddenly yelled to my husband, Clayton. He was affectionately known within our derby world as Mr. Madness. My friend Michelle stopped, too. She skated under the handle "Her Meechness." She had these amazing, long, strong legs that made her an asset to our team. They both froze, looking at me to figure out what I wanted. "Did you hear that?" I whispered.

"Meew."

There it was! Oh, it was so small. That was the precious, squeaky sound of a newborn cat. We moved softly to the east wall of our building and waited for one more.

"Meew."

There it was again, the sound of a tiny new kitten, coming through the half-a-century-old brick and mortar. We stopped unloading the truck and instantly became a Roller Derby kitty rescue team. This kitty needed our help. As the team medic, that is what I do—I respond to those who need me, whether on the track or, now, in the alley.

But where exactly was this cat? In the wall? Yes, and we were on the other side of the wall, separated by a long enclosed alley. To get there we'd have to move a gigantic sliding steel door that had come off its rusty old track. It took all three of us to muscle that heavy steel door open enough for one of us to slide through. It made a horrible scraping noise on the concrete floor. We stopped. There was silence.

"Meew."

It was still there! Slightly louder now, letting us know of its whereabouts. I slid through and was in the alley, surrounded by almost pitch blackness at first. My eyes adjusted. I felt along the cobweb-covered wall. There were no lights. The dim afternoon haze thru the cracks in the roofline was no help.

There were two white, midsize industrial trucks parked in the alley. They came into view quickly and I recognized them as belonging to our neighboring business. It was a tight fit, a shimmy to squeeze by, and I got dusty webs on my clothes as I brushed against the wall. I could hear Michelle as she was sliding along the same wall, following me on this rescue mission.

We had not heard a sound for a few minutes. I made my way down the alley, softly calling out, "Kitty, kitty, kitty." I hoped we weren't too late…. Finally, there it was. One final sound was all we needed to locate our target.

"Meew."

Just behind an oddly shaped alcove in the alley was

a very slight, very hungry jet-black kitten. As I later discovered, a girl. She seemed hesitant to emerge from the wall, but she was curious. She did not object as I reached into the wall for her. She was so small. She looked at me with her green eyes. I might have been the first human she'd ever seen.

I snuggled her against my shirt. We shimmied our way back down the alley to the steel door and slid through. Once back in the well-lit warehouse, we did a full survey. She was darling. There were no apparent injuries, but yes, a flea or two. And now that she'd been rescued, she would not stop talking.

"Meew, meew, meew, meew!"

It was a constant flow of sound, like an infant's attempt at communicating. It was as if the kitten was saying, "This baby needs to be fed and bathed! Prompt attention please!"

Scrambling around the warehouse and rummaging through our cars, we found a few things. Kitty was placed in a cardboard box with a soft blanket and some water. The water spilled within moments as she wanted to leap and jump and play. She was so small, we were afraid she would get wedged in another nook in the warehouse. So we closed the box and watched it hippity-hop around the floor as she objected to her confinement.

We'd all planned to work on the building that

afternoon, but now those plans were canceled. I loaded up our impatient orphan and took her home. Once she was bathed and cleaned up, she settled right in with a litter box and some food. It was time to search for a loving family. I love cats, but I already had two. A third addition was not a wise option. Someone else would have to be persuaded to take this kitty in.

I thought of a solution. Another Roller Derby girl, Tiffany, with raven-black hair and the skate name Pink Devil, had a penchant for wayward animals. A dog with one ear and a kitten with one eye were just two of now five animals that shared her home. Maybe she needed a tiny black kitten…. I convinced her to come over for a visit. I was certain if I could just get her to meet this little wallflower, she would be smitten. Unfairly, I cajoled her with text message pictures and tales of the kitten's rescue.

She responded quickly, and soon enough we were all three sitting on the floor of the garage. I watched Tiffany and the new kitten interact. She'd recently lost a beloved pet, and it was clear she was quite taken with the midnight-colored feline. Our gentle little rescue walked over to her adoptive mom and climbed into her lap, snuggling into the folds of her skirt. I described her rescue from the wall the day before, and Tiffany nodded in approval as I detailed how we had all moved the steel door together. She stroked the kitten as I talked.

"So," I asked gently, hoping to seal the deal, "what do you want to name her?"

"Well, it is October," she said. "She is black as night. Her day of rescue is very fitting. We shall call her Wednesday."

Hammer

As Told to Morton Rumberg

This is the story of Hammer. He was unconscious when I met him for the first time. Our animal control officer had seized five pit bulls, charging their owner with being an unfit caretaker and with cruelty to animals. The house they lived in had been condemned because of accumulated filth, debris and fecal matter. The animal control officer took the dogs to a veterinarian for examination. Four were young dogs: one young male, a breeding female and two young females. They were moderately to severely underweight, filthy, and infested with fleas, hookworms and whipworms. The male had numerous bite scars, especially on his legs and head, but all the dogs were friendly and surprisingly trusting. And then there was Hammer.

Hammer was attached to a short, thick chain that could easily be used to tow a truck. The chain weighed twenty-seven pounds. The spike anchoring the chain to the ground weighed another ten pounds. Hammer was the guard dog, the fierce protector of the only home he knew. The owner said that he had to keep Hammer chained because he was so aggressive. Hammer had to be tranquilized to enable the veterinarian to examine him safely.

Hammer was a pit bull; a large, full-grown, heavy-boned dog, but he weighed only fifty pounds. Every part of his body was witness to the hell his life had been. The details were grim. He was emaciated—every rib, every bone in his spine was clearly visible. Bite scars were visible all over his body. His ears, severely cut in the "fighting crop," were swollen, inflamed and badly infected. A fist-sized growth, probably an untreated tumor, protruded from his side, and several smaller tumors were located elsewhere on his body, including in his groin area. He had an open abscess on his front leg.

His entire abdominal area was blackened from a long-term, untreated bacterial infection. His neck and throat were raw, inflamed and infected from pulling against the chain. He had an unforgettable rank odor of filth and infection. His canine teeth were broken, and all his other teeth were worn down almost to the gums, probably from chewing on the chain. It was impossible to estimate his age, given the condition of his teeth and his overall physical condition. He could be anywhere from five to fifteen years of age. That was Hammer.

Their veterinary exams completed, the dogs arrived at the shelter. I carried Hammer, still unconscious, to a run that I'd padded with blankets to keep him from hurting himself when he awoke from the tranquilizer. Through that long evening the youngsters were photographed, vaccinated, dewormed, bathed and dipped. They accepted it all trustingly. And then there was Hammer.

The shelter staff checked on him often as he began to wake up. He followed our every move, as if he was trying to understand what was happening. Finally, we finished our initial care for the youngsters, but we hadn't vaccinated Hammer. Even the friendliest dogs can be unpredictable as they're waking from anesthesia. Common sense said to forget it, and just leave him alone, but that was not our way. One staff member held Hammer's head in a bear hug while another vaccinated him. He barely struggled and we began to wonder how vicious he really was.

Our animal control officers, the veterinarians and the Commonwealth attorney did an outstanding job putting the case together against the dogs' owner. The court upheld our petition to have the owner declared unfit to provide proper care for the dogs, and awarded their custody to the animal shelter. A few weeks later, in criminal court, the owner entered a plea of guilty to the charge of animal cruelty. But the wheels of justice moved slowly and the dogs would be with us until the case was finally closed.

Meanwhile, at the shelter the dogs had been put on a special feeding regimen for malnutrition. Hammer's food was laced with antibiotics for his many infections. All five dogs gained weight steadily and their condition visibly improved from day to day. The youngsters were friendly with everyone on staff. And then there was Hammer.

Hammer would jump on his cage door as people approached, barking with his distinctive deep, yet hoarse voice. He used his food and water bowls as Frisbees, shaking and tossing them around. We gave him heavy, tip-proof water and food bowls and a thick rope toy to shake. He demolished the frame of his metal dog door one day by constantly barreling into it. He didn't want to stay outside during inside cleanup or be inside when we cleaned the outside. His weight and his strength improved daily, but his ears needed topical medication on a regular basis and his skin needed medicated baths. He still smelled horribly.

As lead officer for Hammer, I visited him after hours, when the shelter was quiet, plied him with dog biscuits and talked to him, trying to earn his trust one step at a time. It took a while, but I finally was able to pet him through the bars, then enter the kennel with him and finally medicate his ears. He began to trust me and it was a wonderful feeling.

One night I put a slip lead around his neck and led him through the empty shelter to the grooming room. I invited him to jump in the tub. He had no idea what to expect. The next step could be dangerous. I reached under him to pick him up. Would he let me? We were both surprised it went so smoothly when I placed him in the tub. He looked very warily at me when I turned on the hose, but he let the warm water cascade over him. Owners sometimes encouraged aggression by turning a hose on their dogs, so I was alert to any sudden move he might make, but he put up with it. Perhaps he understood I was trying to help him. He grunted and groaned with delight as he was lathered and massaged, turning different parts of his body toward me for more massaging. The next thing I knew, his huge front paws were on my shoulders and this fierce guard dog was giving me sloppy doggy kisses. I had a new friend named Hammer.

One by one he learned to know and trust several other staff members. We gave each of the pit bull youngsters big rawhide bones. They devoured them in record time. Hammer's teeth were so worn down that he couldn't really chew his, but he loved to carry it around. We began taking him to our fenced exercise area after hours. At first he'd run a few feet and stop, expecting to be jerked back by his chain. Little by little he began to explore and leap and run. When we called him, he would run to us for belly rubs, rolling in the grass on his back, giving us big openmouthed groans of pleasure. He didn't know how to fetch or play with toys, but he loved the attention and the freedom. He continued to gain weight, soon weighing in at sixty-two pounds, with no protruding bones and a shining coat. He was enjoying his new life.

Too soon the final date for the owner to appeal the court ruling arrived. The following day we held Hammer's head tenderly while we euthanized him— his story could end no other way. He was what he was: a large, powerful dog who had been taught to fight other dogs and distrust people. This disqualified him from ever being adopted. At the shelter we had a friend named Hammer. We're proud that we were able to let him know love and trust and simply enjoy being a dog, if only for a short time. We're proud, too, of our other animals, the ones adopted by loving families.

This is what we do. Everyone who works at an animal shelter has stories like Hammer's. Our work may not be understood or appreciated. We do it for the animals because we are all they have. We take them in, give them food, a clean place to live and medical care when they need it. We try to place them with people who have a lifetime of love and care to give. We enjoy them for the time we have with them, and when we say goodbye, whatever the circumstances, we say it with love. We may never change the system or society or the world, but if we continue to care and to take pride in what we do, we *can* make a difference—one day, one animal, one life at a time.

Quiet Vigil

Sue Pearson

She stands in the corner, looking out on the road. This is the only spot in the field that isn't shaded by large, sheltering, beckoning trees. The sun is beating down on her tired body. Her haunches are hollow, with skin stretched tight over hip bones that protrude. Her back is swayed. Her shoulders are bony. Her head is bowed. She stands and she waits.

"Have you noticed that skinny horse in the pasture along the road to your house?" My neighbor and I sometimes run into each other at the feed store, and today she was concerned about this sad-looking horse standing in the blazing sun with its head hung down, looking forlorn and neglected.

I know this horse. Our lives are intertwined. The

story is very different than it appears. To be sure, there is suffering, but along the way there is an invitation to trust in a higher power—a chance to experience the nearness of God. Shiloh and I both have been touched by grace, our paths connected by some divine guidance.

Spiritual growth is often difficult, and this chapter in my growth began when a health crisis sidelined me from a successful career as a journalist and pushed me into early retirement. Friends said, "Just stay at home and play with your horses." And while that sounded appealing, it also sounded a bit self-centered. An organization called Wonder, Inc., offered a chance to make a difference, not in the world or even in my community, but in just one life…the life of a child in foster care.

And so I became a mentor to MJ, an eight-year-old with hair the color of wheat, eyes that sparkled, a personality that said, "I can and I will" again and again. It's the quality the people in child protective services call resilience, and MJ has it. Her enthusiasm won my heart. "When can we start having adventures?" "Can you teach me anything?" "I love to learn!" I explained to MJ that, according to the rules, I had to have three home visits before we could start going out and doing things together. Each time I came over, I brought what I thought were interesting craft projects for us to do in her foster home, things like egg decorating, scrapbooking and beadwork. She dove into each project but didn't have much to say. Where had the earlier excitement gone?

"Is there anything on your mind, MJ?" I asked.

"Yes, there is," she said. "When can we get outta here and start having fun?"

"Okay. Next time, I promise, we can get out of here and start having fun." I laughed. I told her a little bit about myself. "I have five children—one girl, four boys—and mostly they are grown and gone from home. In six months my youngest boy will graduate from high school and leave for college."

MJ threw back her head and turned to me, her long ponytail flicking from side to side. "Well, aren't you lucky to have me now!"

I laughed at her spunkiness. Looking back, this was the moment I fell in love with her, certain a lifetime bond was in the making.

We went to plays, concerts, the zoo, skipped rocks at the river, hiked in the mountains, played with my dog; and when a neighbor offered to loan me her child-safe pony, I gave MJ riding lessons. I knew from my long years of riding and caring for horses that these animals offered an extraordinary learning experience. In honing good equestrian skills, a lot of pretty amazing life skills get formed and sharpened. Things like leadership, patience, responsibility, self-confidence and more. MJ was a little scared when she first got on Diamond, but with slow and steady guidance from me, she was ready for her first horse show within eight months. We borrowed show clothes, and together we groomed Diamond until the pony gleamed.

In the show arena, I had to let go of MJ. No more helping. She was on her own now. I leaned against the arena fence, drumming my fingers nervously on the top rail. I must have held my breath the entire time, because when the judge announced the results, with MJ awarded first place, the air came rushing out of my lungs in one huge whooping shout of joy. The smile on MJ's face could have lit up the universe. I was helping her with what is all too often missing in the life of a foster child—the opportunity to thrive. The surprise was how much she gave back to me. I felt energized and needed.

Suddenly MJ was at a crossroads. From her social workers she learned she would either return to her biological mother, be put up for adoption or stay in foster care until she aged out of the system at eighteen. Every option seemed scary. While the unknown was looming, the thing MJ was most concerned about was me. I had indeed filled the role Wonder, Inc. had intended—to be a constant presence, the one who followed through on promises and offered a fount of unconditional love.

"I'm worried we won't be able to be together." The usually upbeat MJ was somber.

I did my best to reassure her. "Honey, as far as I'm

concerned, I'm with you for life. Even if you get tired of me someday, you'll have a hard time getting rid of me." I hoped she would smile but she didn't. It's hard to trust when trust has been broken. I knew I would hang in there no matter what, but MJ wasn't so sure.

In a matter of weeks MJ's mother lost her parental rights, and thus going home was no longer an option for MJ. Social workers sought to find a family who would adopt her, and three times she was moved. I saw MJ try her hardest to bond with the new parents, accept different rules, adjust to new schools, find new friends and just fit in. But every time she did these things, she was expected to do it all over again somewhere else.

The people who study the effects of the foster-care system on children say these kids experience more post-traumatic stress than war vets. Having now seen it up close, I understand.

Through each move I stayed connected, though the foster families lived many hours away. MJ told me she had high hopes for the second foster home. "The room they had fixed up for me was so pretty. I thought I could be happy there." When I visited after the third move and took her out to lunch, she was desperately unhappy.

At the noisy café, she leaned in close and said, "I told myself to just hang on, because I knew when you got here, you would make everything all right. Get me back to the other family quick, okay?"

I choked back tears. "Oh, MJ, I don't have these magical powers. I can't make everything all right. The only thing I can do is be your friend and love you through all the good times and bad times. I will hug you when you are sad. I will listen when you need to talk. I will be your cheerleader for life. Someday you are going to have a life of your own design and it's going to be wonderful." Now we were two broken hearts. Hers because I wasn't the hero she wanted me to be. Mine because I had to take away that illusion. I cried most of the way home.

Later I made plans with a stable near MJ to bring our borrowed pony for day trips so she could continue her riding lessons. I began to map out a routine and dream up new adventures. I knew there were some problems in the new family and that MJ was not doing well in school. I thought the foster-care people would give this patched-together family time to work everything out. I was wrong. The director of Wonder called. "Sorry to have to tell you this, but MJ has been moved yet again, and I don't have the new contact information. We'll just have to be patient."

What! Be patient? Are you kidding? I couldn't believe what I had just heard. Four moves in six months! I was angry. How could a system meant to protect these children bring so much additional trauma into their lives by shuffling them around? MJ was in a state of perpetual emotional whiplash. No one should have to endure this chaos, much less our vulnerable, powerless children. This time I wanted to shake things up…take some people down…bring the system to a reckoning. I vowed to call on my journalism skills to right this obvious wrong.

But the assault on the system would have to wait until Monday. Some weeks before, I had signed up to spend that weekend at a spiritual retreat, a monastery in the mountains, looking out over the sea. Within the first few hours I felt a tremendous calling. I kept sensing a message…. *Be quiet. Lose the anger. Wait without judgment.* But what was happening to MJ and so many other foster children was just wrong. Something should be done. Then that message again. *Be still. Be open.* I listened. As hard as it was, I shed the anger and the judgment. I would hold a quiet vigil, because I had made a decision to trust this piercing message.

Monday afternoon the director of Wonder, Inc. called me. "MJ has a new foster home and guess where it is." Well, it could have been anywhere in the state. I wasn't in the mood for games. So to be flippant, I spat out the name of the unlikeliest place—the tiny country hamlet where I lived.

"Yes!" the director said. "That's where MJ's new home is."

"Don't be kidding around with me," I said.

"No, no kidding. In fact she lives just down the street from you," he replied.

God winked. I am sure of it. I was deeply humbled.

Three years have passed since I heeded God's message to lose the anger and wait. MJ is flourishing in a stable family with a foster mom and dad who have good values and great parenting skills. They, and I, are committed to helping MJ succeed in life. She is doing well in school and has joined the ranks of preteens everywhere, with girlfriends, sleepovers and a lot of giggling.

A few months ago she and I went to visit a friend of mine who operates a horse rescue center nearby—a place called the Grace Foundation. My friend, Beth, knew of my mentoring journey with MJ. She said, "If you are ready to adopt a horse, I have one I have been saving for just the perfect home. MJ, would you like to meet Shiloh?"

And that is how Shiloh came to live in the front pasture at MJ's house. The horse had been badly neglected, starved and left in a barren field to die. MJ is taking excellent care of her horse, giving her plenty of good hay and clean water. The horse is groomed and stroked tenderly every day. MJ rides her on a nearby trail or bareback in the front field. Shiloh and MJ have a bond. They both know about betrayal and hardship.

The mare trots across the field in the morning as MJ walks from her house to the bus stop. It's not far.

In the corner where the fencing meets, the horse can see her best friend being taken away in a big, noisy yellow box. She has no idea where. But she is willing to suffer the searing heat of the sun to wait there for MJ. Shiloh trusts her quiet vigil will end when her friend is returned in the afternoon. A passage from the Bible frames this scene: "In silence and in hope will be your strength."

As MJ steps from the bus and walks along the fence line to the house, the horse trots from the corner to the other end of the pasture to follow her home. They both have learned that love is worth waiting for. So have I.

A Life Measured in Dog Years

Hal Bernton

I married into the basset-hound breed.

One day in Twin Falls, Idaho, after running the Snake River Canyon from rim to rim, I met a slender, young woman at a post-race picnic. Her basset hound grabbed the sandwich in my hand, and the owner, Ann, soon claimed my heart.

That was more than twenty-five years ago. Since then, Ann and I have shared many memorable moments with the gentle, long-eared, keen-nosed and often stubborn hounds.

There were bassets at our wedding and one on our honeymoon.

When my newspaper career took us north to Alaska for eleven years, our bassets joined us as we hiked through grizzly country, fished for salmon and picked fall berries in alpine meadows. In one memorable experiment, we briefly hitched our bootee-clad basset, Homer, to an Iditarod racer's sled for a pull through the snow. But bassets as sled dogs never quite caught on.

When we moved to the Pacific Northwest, Ann decided she wanted to check out field trials, which give your hound a chance to match his scent and tracking skills against other bassets. We joined a small, eclectic band of basset-hound brethren who have kept field trialing alive in our region. Most come from Washington and Oregon, and a handful from as far away as Idaho and California.

These dogs were initially bred in France as low-slung hounds that could help hunters pursue small game. The field trials are a way to honor this hunting heritage. The trials are held along a stretch of land in southwest Washington that is piled with Mount St. Helens's ash dredged from a nearby river. This land has been reclaimed by a motley mix of Scotch broom, Himalayan blackberries and grasses, all of which provide prime cover for rabbits.

These competitions typically begin soon after daybreak. Most participants form a line, known as "the Gallery," and walk forward slowly, beating the bushes with sticks or poles in hopes of flushing out a bunny. Eventually, someone cries "Tallyho!" as a rabbit scurries out of the brush. Then two bassets are walked up to the point where the bunny was last seen. They are left on the bunny's trail for several minutes. That's enough time for two judges to decide which of the dogs does a better job of following the scent. (Hunting is forbidden at field trialing, and bassets are bred to flush out game, rather than track it down and pounce on it. And the dogs are caught and leashed long before they would have the chance to catch and harm the rabbits they pursue.)

At first, field trialing didn't hook me. I thought the people were too intense and the pace was awfully slow, and many of the dogs often were surprisingly uninterested in following the rabbit scents. My dog, Winston, was a complete bust and finished far back in the pack. But Ann was not ready to give up on Winston. She was convinced he eventually would figure things out. He had been born at a humble kennel in Oregon's Willamette Valley, one that had not produced any renowned field-trial dogs. But on our walks and weekend outings, Winston always had his nose to the ground, so Ann was convinced his mythical "lightbulb," which one of our field-trial friends had talked about, would turn on.

It did. After a few field trials, Ann took Winston up to the point where the rabbit was first spotted. He inhaled deeply and began to howl. A wild, exuberant howl that he repeated again and again as he sniffed his way through the field. Winston took a red ribbon that day. In the months and years that followed, he won enough ribbons to gain the title of a champion. In 2008 he finally had enough placements to reach the highest level of achievement—grand field champion.

All this was not accomplished without controversy. Judges assess the dogs on a number of traits, such as desire, determination, endurance and "proper use of voice." Winston had plenty of critics who thought he was too quick to howl. Some called him a babbler who somehow fooled the judges by howling when he didn't really, truly smell a rabbit. Over time, the criticism eased, even if it did not fade entirely, as Winston aged and grew more refined in his approach. He would move more slowly, bark less often, and he once successfully followed a rabbit's scent across a difficult stretch of sandy roadway.

There was plenty of competitive fervor at the field trials, sometimes too much, as a few nasty disputes flared up. There was also romance. Though most of the field trialers were well into their fifties, sixties or even seventies, one younger couple began their courtship while tramping through tall creek-side grass in search of rabbits. They ended up getting married. We all attended their wedding ceremony, held after a long day of field trialing. There were also sad moments. Some dogs died. Some field trialers died, and we tried to honor their passing by ensuring their dogs—brought down by surviving spouses—continued to compete.

In the spring of 2010 Winston was diagnosed with a blood cancer. Over the summer he gradually faded away. He would bleed internally, then regain strength and then bleed again. On our twenty-fifth wedding anniversary Ann and I went to stay at a hotel in the Columbia River Gorge. Winston was so weak that he had to be wheeled on the luggage cart to our room. He passed away the next day, and we buried him in our backyard.

Ann said she wouldn't get another basset for at least a year. The illness had been so long and drawn out, and she wasn't ready for another basset. She was upset that we had even tried to leave home on our anniversary. But it was awfully quiet at our house. Our two children had both left for college. At night it was just the two of us, and a lot of basset memories.

Last October I was driving down Interstate 5 near the basset-hound field-trial grounds. I realized there was a competition that weekend and stopped by to say hello. Everyone offered condolences about Winston's passing. Then a friend suggested we consider adopting a two-year-old basset named Maverick. He had spent two months with a family in Oregon. Things hadn't worked out, and he had just been returned to the kennel of his birth. Maverick had beautiful lines and those soulful basset eyes. He came right up to me at the field-trial grounds and put his paws on my lap. I gave him a hug and took a bunch of cell phone pictures of the dog to show Ann.

Today, Maverick is a much-loved member of our family, although we think he sometimes struggles with our suburban lifestyle. Maverick had lived most of his puppyhood at a wonderful place, Tailgate Ranch Kennels on Whidbey Island, where he spent his days playing in the fields with his siblings. He was a country boy, and he initially seemed a bit insecure. He frequently sought to jump in our laps or snuggle up against us as we sat on the couch. And he could be spooked by small things, such as the sound of rattling paper.

But he was passionate about hunting. That made walking a chore, as he strained on his leash and often refused to move past a promising scent of a squirrel or cat. So in the spring we brought Maverick to the field trials. In his first competition he was a dud, just like Winston had been. But the second time around, he came to the line and gave a howl. Then another and another as he raced off through the Scotch broom.

The Green Collar

Sheryl J. Bize Boutte

Dogs were not among my mother's favorite things.
Begged for and then promptly neglected by each of her
five daughters, or promising and then failed watchdogs
for my father, they were just an extra chore for my
mother. On more than one occasion she would yell
from some corner of the house, "If you don't feed that
dog, you are going to find him stiff in the backyard!"
Sometimes that threat would propel one of her girls
into action, but more often, the playdate or the telephone call or the party would take precedence and the
dog du jour's stay at our house would come to an end.

So it came as a complete and utter shock to all of
us when one day in 1980, my mother came home with
a fluffy brilliantly white toy poodle she had already
named Pierre.

Somehow this Pierre had managed to break through

Mom's decades-long avoidance of all things dog and capture her heart. Her devotion to him was proven even more when, at scarcely three months old, he required a serious and expensive operation. We thought for sure he would be counted among the "temporary" dogs we had growing up, but again to our surprise, Mom took him to the vet hospital, paid the bill without a word and walked the floor during his surgery as though he were one of her children. It was clear that Mom and Pierre had a special bond, and looking back, I think even he knew it.

Pierre fit perfectly into Mom's life at that point. At a moment when her children sometimes placed conditions on giving her time and attention, Pierre was constant and unwavering in his loyalty. He asked no questions, never talked back and did not have any other obligations. He was calm, quiet and stealthily present, an escape from the sometimes raucous sibling rivalry, which often shattered mom's peace. He looked her in the eyes when she spoke to him and seemed to listen and understand. It was as though their destinies had been divinely intertwined by forces beyond our control or understanding. And even though he was "Mom's dog," he was always happy to see us and, acting as the perfect host, greeted us warmly when we arrived at the front door to the family home.

Then, in 1981, at the young age of fifty-three and

scarcely a year after bringing Pierre home, my mother died suddenly. The shocking loss of the person who was literally the glue that held us together created a fracture in our family that has never been mended. Pierre grieved along with us during those dark days of turning off life support and during the heavy emptiness that followed. Like us he shunned food, looked for her in the house and inhaled the lingering scent of Youth-Dew in her clothes to invoke her presence. During this time, Pierre transitioned from Mom's beloved pet to the living vessel in which memories of her were stored.

When my father could no longer live with the memories that filled the house he had shared with my mother, he took Pierre with him to his new house and later to a small apartment, after the last of my sisters got married and moved away. The cramped apartment soon became too small for the lively and energetic Pierre. It was then that Pierre came to live with my husband, my young daughter and me.

Struggling against the leash my father held, freshly groomed and decorated with a new bright green collar, Pierre pranced across the threshold of our front door. After greeting the three of us, he ran through his new home, exploring each room. While it was understood that Pierre had an extended family, it was also clear that he would live out the rest of his days with us. During the ensuing years, Pierre kept my mom ever present and brought us joy, calm and unfettered, pure devotion. His regard for us enhanced our regard for each other. He was regal and anointed, with the countenance of a true gentleman.

With his seven pounds of assumed swagger, he ruled his backyard kingdom, protecting it from raccoon, cat or bird interlopers who dared to set foot on his hallowed turf. He could jump three times his height and never licked a face without permission. We laughed when he would bare his teeth and bark to protect us from strangers or perceived harm. When an acquaintance came to visit and unkindly referred to him as a "little rat," he was forever banned from our home.

No matter the season, when the sun would reach a certain point in the sky, Pierre would use his nose to turn over his bowl, signaling he was ready to eat. The sound of the electric can opener would send him bounding into the kitchen in anticipation of food. He loved to ride in the car, running from the back to the front and to the back again, never disturbing the driver. He luxuriated in bubble baths and would turn over without prompting for the soothing heat of the blow-dryer. And while he was undemanding and patient, he was every inch the proud and high-stepping poodle. He was happiest after grooming and would throw his head and shoulders back and strut with the bearing of a lion.

When I used my air popper to make popcorn, Pierre

would scoop up the flying kernels from the kitchen floor. (To this day, when I use that air popper and have to get the broom to sweep up the errant kernels, my husband and I will say in unison, "Where is Pierre when we need him?") When we needed a hug, Pierre would place his face on our shoulder, and we could almost hear him tell us everything would be all right. Pierre was our unruffled constant when we needed it most.

In 1995 it became clear that Pierre's health was failing. By then he was seventy-six in dog years and had lost sight in one eye and most of his teeth. He was no longer the luminous white ball of boundless energy, but a lethargic, yellowing shadow of himself. As it had happened many years before with my mother, it became clear that life was leaving him and we had to make a decision.

So while our daughter, who could not bear to say goodbye, packed the rented minivan we were using to drive her to college, my husband and I took Pierre for his last car ride to the vet. The vet took one look at Pierre and told us his time had come. On a hot August day, on what would have been my mother's sixty-ninth birthday, my husband and I tearfully removed Pierre's green collar and said our goodbyes.

We drove home in silence. There were no words. We immersed ourselves in the other life-changing event before us: our daughter leaving home for her freshman year of college. We had planned it this way on purpose so we would not have time to dwell on the loss of Pierre. We were forced to focus on what was ahead.

There is no doubt in my mind that Pierre came at the right time for all of us. For my mom, he was the one who doted on her when all others seemed to have fallen away. And during what turned out to be the last year of Mom's short life, Pierre gave her the gift of unconditional love. For the rest of us, Pierre was the only thing that remained calm and steady after she died, a time of family upheaval and change. He filled a void that would have been left open and unresolved. He was a connection to my mother that we all needed to keep from falling off the cliff. He was also an entity unto himself, independently loved and cherished.

Every now and then, I open the desk drawer in the kitchen and look at the green collar. It still contains small tufts of Pierre's fur. After all these years I am still amazed at the power this ten-inch slash of fabric has to evoke such strong emotion and vivid recollection. Holding it in my hand starts the video of Pierre gazing up at Mom. Then, as the camera is pulled back and the image widens, Mom's smiling face comes into the frame. As a physical manifestation of memory, the collar provides the tangible closeness Mom and I always shared and I continue to need.

I could stretch out the green collar and encase it in a frame. I could hang it from my rearview mirror or have it sewn into a quilt. But I prefer to keep it unencumbered but latched, as if to form the halo I am sure still floats above Pierre's head.

Growing Together

Louise Crawford

When I first met my dog Lily, she was living with a foster-dog mom. I drove about an hour to get to the foster home, intending to meet a short-haired, small black dog that would fit my house and my backyard. However, when the foster-doggy mom opened the door, my eyes were drawn to another dog, which stood amid this herd of barking dogs, not making a peep.

She just stared up at me with her big brown eyes and trembled. This dog was clearly terrified, and so was I. I felt an instant sympathetic bond, but what if she wasn't a dog looking for a home? What if she belonged to the household? And what if I really wasn't ready for this dog ownership step?

"What can you tell me about this one?" I asked the woman in charge, pointing at the orange-and-white, fluffy-eared sweetie. "Is that your dog or a foster dog?"

She looked down at the trembling dog. "Her? Oh, she's new. Just came in. We haven't even gotten her photo up on the website yet. We're calling her Lily."

My heart leapt, and I blurted, "That's the dog I want!"

Immediately I regretted saying it. The thought of having my own dog and being completely responsible for it was something I was really struggling with. Yes, I know most of the world is at ease with the idea of owning a pet, but not me. It had taken me three years in counseling to get to this point. My childhood was a hard one, and the aftereffects have left me with serious issues of self-worth, particularly when it comes to doing or having something that is just for me. Not for others, just for me. A dog would be just for me, and secretly I still wondered whether I deserved that.

When I bent down to get closer, I noticed one of Lily's ribs poked out and she shook in terror. Had she been mistreated, too? I didn't try to pet her but just stayed still. She was so small. I looked up at the foster mom. "What kind of dog is Lily?"

"The vet thinks she's part papillon and part Chihuahua," she said. With a laugh, she added, "Her ears could be from either breed."

Lily's ears reminded me of a fruit bat's. They stood up like two radar dishes on the top of her head, alert for any threatening sound. This was not a dog that would relax and trust easily.

At the foster mom's suggestion I went to the couch and sat down. Within minutes Lily had jumped up and settled on my lap. It was love. This was the dog I wanted. Because Lily was so new, I couldn't take her with me that day. I had paperwork to complete, and she needed to be spayed and have a tracking chip implanted so she'd never get lost again.

I stayed and stroked Lily's soft fur, hating to leave her there. Then I went home and told my daughter happily, "I found a dog!" I'd initially wanted a short-haired dog that wouldn't shed, but once I met Lily, I didn't care if I had dog hair all over my house, or if my house smelled like "furry animals."

It became more obvious that Lily had been mistreated, as well as abandoned, when my daughter and I drove out to pick her up the next week. Lily still didn't make a sound, while all the other dogs barked in excitement at the door. This time I noticed the poky rib again and how she retreated when I came near her, then nipped at me when I tried to pet her, letting me know I was moving too fast.

I sat on the couch with my daughter and the foster mom, and we chatted while Lily slowly gathered her courage and came into the room. After a few minutes she jumped up onto the couch between my daughter and me. We both let her smell us and finally she let us pet her.

Armed with dog food, a book on dog behavior and the name of a vet for emergencies, we drove home. Little Lily rested on a soft green blanket on my daughter's lap. She poked her head up once in a while to peer out the window, but other than that, she stayed put and made no sound. Once we were home, I put Lily's blanket on a small beanbag chair in the living room. It was meant to be her bed. She lay down on it, her eyes wide with fear, her little body shaking, and didn't move all evening. Before bedtime I took her into the backyard and she peed. Then I brought her back inside and she slept on her bed all night.

I planned to do this right—I wasn't going to just plop a dog in my house and expect it all to work. I'd taken a week's vacation from work so we could get to know each other. Our first day I hung out with her and watched her explore the house. When I sat on the couch to watch TV, she sat next to me. That night she slept on the couch instead of her bed.

I'd never imagined I would let a dog sleep on the couch, or anywhere except on its bed or in its crate, but here I was, happy to let her sleep on the double recliner. I stood in the doorway, smiling down at the sleeping dog. This adorable little fluff ball, all curled up in the corner of the armrest was my watchdog! *Life would be perfect,* I thought, *now that I have a dog to call my own.*

But the next morning Lily wheezed and coughed

like she was trying to cough up a hair ball. She sounded like she might die. What had gone wrong already? What didn't I do right? Terrified, I put her in her crate and drove to the vet. She whimpered and clawed and cried the entire drive, which was horrendous, because it was New Year's Eve and the traffic was awful. It took an hour to get there. She was scratching to get out of the crate, crying and coughing like I was the meanest owner in the world, and her new mom was a basket case.

You know what they say about owners? That if the dog has a problem, treat the owner. Well, I think the vet saw that I was not coping well: my tears and my statement "I think my dog's dying!" clued her in. She ushered Lily and me into a room, came in and calmed us both down, then took Lily in the back to examine her. By the time she placed Lily back in my arms, I was no longer hyperventilating or crying.

"Lily has kennel cough and needs antibiotics," the lady vet said, smiling reassuringly. "I'll give her a prescription, and you can pay for it out front."

As I held this warm, wonderful fluff ball in my arms, I realized that in my panic, I'd left my purse, my wallet and, most important, my Visa card at home. I tried calling home, but my daughter wasn't there, so after being reassured Lily would be fine, I drove home with her, got her settled and drove back to the vet to pay for the medicine. Happy New Year!

The next few days I watched Lily anxiously, waiting for her cough to go away. The first sign she felt better, and safer, was when she went to the front window and barked at a passing car. This was Lily's first bark! For a little dog, she had a fierce bark, but I didn't want her barking all day, so I encouraged her to go to the window and look out before barking, using my voice and treats.

During the week I was home, I worked with her, teaching her to sit, lift her paw and shake, and "dance." She liked dancing for treats best! I'm currently playing fetch with her and teaching her the commands "jump" and "down." She taught me, as well. After she spent a couple of nights on the couch, when her cough worried me, I put her doggy blanket on a chair next to my bed and let her sleep there. After two more nights, she was sleeping on the end of my bed, then right beside me, curled up in the small of my back or the crook of my legs. At first I worried that I might injure her when I moved in my sleep, but I quickly learned that if I moved, she moved. She was quite adept at taking care of herself.

When I took her to a local vet to make sure she was over the kennel cough and to get heartworm and flea medicine, I discovered that Lily seemed terrified of men. One look at the male vet, who was not at all threatening, and she peed on the steel table, shook, then barked. When he tried to put a muzzle on her, she was not having any of that, and I was so traumatized by then, I thanked him and took Lily home. I could see that the two of us both had healing work to do.

In the meantime, I tried to bulk her up. Taking a tip from the movie *As Good as It Gets*—if you ever saw the movie, you may remember the scene where Jack Nicholson feeds bacon to Greg Kinnear's dog—I started adding in a tablespoon of bacon bits to her food. Uh-oh. Big mistake. She loved the bacon, but she also started putting on weight!

When I took her for a six-month checkup to a female vet who had been recommended by a friend and was close to home, the vet told me, "Your dog needs to lose about two pounds." Since I teach weight management classes (as well as write suspense, romance and fantasy fiction), imagine my chagrin at hearing *my* dog was overweight. I worked on eating a healthy, low-fat diet, yet I was feeding my dog bacon. I left the vet's office determined to stop the bacon treats cold turkey and stick to dog food for Lily.

Of course, my resolve nearly crumbled when Lily gave me the biggest sad-eyed stare the next morning, her sweet little face asking, "Where's the bacon?" Oh, dear. This wasn't going to be easy, was it? The vet had warned me, "Small dogs are notoriously good at getting their owners to feed them bad foods," so I steeled myself with the knowledge Lily would live a longer, healthier life if she was fed properly, then went and bought appropriate doggy treats for small dogs, along with some "banquet-style" food made by the same company that made her dry food. I mixed a fourth of the can of wet food in with her dry food twice a day. At first she held off eating, to see if I'd relent and feed her bacon again, but once she accepted the bacon was gone for good, she ate her food—sometimes with a mournful expression. I wonder if after two and a half years, she dreams about bacon?

Over the next few years, Lily and I slowly fell into a routine. We walked about thirty minutes in the morning; then I fed her and went to work. When we first started our walks, Lily barked in warning at every car, person and dog we passed. Gradually, over time, she went from full-out barks to mild warning growls, to curiously sniffing at other dog owners and their dogs in brief "meet and greets."

When I asked my daughter, who was in and out of the house for college classes, what she and Lily did while I was at work, my daughter laughed. "She just sleeps on your bed or your pillow all day, then races to the door when you get home." Before I put my key in the dead bolt, Lily was on the other side of the door, waiting joyously for me to come in, her tail wagging so hard, I thought she'd wag it off, her little body jumping up and down with excitement, and her rather long tongue trying to get a few kisses in when I crouched down to pet her and say hello. She really did become my dog, a dog solely focused on me.

Nothing gets healed overnight, and we both still have scars from our early years. Lily still has one rib that sticks out, perhaps the remnants of a swift kick to the side when she was a small puppy. She is still skittish around strangers. I'm still working to heal emotional wounds from my childhood. But together, Lily and I can focus on the present rather than the past.

The Improbable Cat Lover

Jennifer O'Neill-Pickering

I had always thought of myself as a dog person. This was because of a country upbringing, where our dogs performed double and even triple duties: herding animals, policing the property and serving as a family member before this was fashionable. I didn't grow up with cats that were pets. Cats took care of varmints in the barn.

This changed in my early thirties, when my friend had to choose between her apartment and a kitten that, her landlord said, "wasn't part of the rental agreement." She called on the phone in tears, asking if I'd consider adopting her half-grown cat, Lady.

"Well, I'm not exactly a cat person," I said. "Let me think about it after I meet Lady." We made a date for me to meet her pet the next day.

I sat in her studio apartment, looking down at

Lady, who had already done loopy loops around my pant legs, marking me as part of her territory. *What a sweet cat,* I thought as she jumped in my lap and curled up into a purring ball.

"Well, it looks like someone's already made up her mind," I observed.

The next day I called my friend to say, "Yes, I'd take her." As we drove away, I thought about all the positives of having a cat. People with cats had lower blood pressure, and didn't cat owners live longer than people without felines? I recalled a story my supervisor had shared. Her pet had the habit of using her as a human trampoline and had discovered a lump in her breast, which turned out to be a cancerous tumor. The cat had saved her life. With these thoughts swirling around in my mind, I drove Lady to her new home. My friend had assured me that Lady was not a "hunter" and that no "feathered" or "furry" gifts would be deposited on my front porch or on bed pillows. Thankfully, she was correct in this prediction.

When Lady first came home, she stepped right out of her crate, walking like she had just graduated from kitty-cat charm school. She jumped up on my favorite living room wingback chair, a queen on her throne. She was stubborn and wasn't going to give up the chair. If I sat in it, she'd join me and then climb on its top and pretend she was a warm scarf, wrapping around my neck and shoulders. I decided she might need her own chair and so I bought another—for myself. She also decided quickly that the bed was a more comfortable place to sleep than the cat bed I'd provided. If she slept on the bed, she deserved a soft pillow to spin dreams on.

She was called Lady because she walked like a lady in four dainty white boots. These contrasted with her jet-black coat and the white diamond pinned on her chest. She also could have been named Diamond. Her eyes were almond shaped and the color of amber and seemed to read minds. Chatty might have been another suitable name for Lady, because she always had something to say and talked nonstop from the moment I stepped through the door.

She was quite the social butterfly, which was a surprise, because I'd read cats were solitary in nature and territorial. Not true of Lady. She had two neighborhood chums: a rotund tabby and an enormous Russian blue. The pride liked to hang out on top of the garage and watch the goings-on of the neighborhood. Each night, when I pulled into the driveway, Lady greeted me feetfirst, jumping on the hood of my car from the roof of the garage.

Eventually, I met a wonderful man and we bought a house in a new neighborhood. Lady was not pleased and sulked in one of the bedrooms for several days. She finally forgave us and quickly claimed her new space, marking all the furniture and doorjambs about the house. We did not yet have a cat door, but Lady soon adapted. One evening, as we sat with friends over glasses of wine, there came a knock at the door, followed by another.

"Are you expecting more guests?" one of our friends asked.

"Yes, just one," I replied. "Would one of you mind getting the door?"

Before one of them could reach the door, there was another knock.

"Whoever it is, is impatient," said our friend who'd offered to get the door. She opened the door, and there sat Lady, one paw lifted behind the screen door, ready to "knock" again.

Lady stopped, looked up with blinking amber eyes that asked, "What took you so long?"

Not long afterward, we introduced a new cat into our family, Mr. Peach. Lady soon taught him to knock on the door, too.

My husband was a musician and a music teacher. We had a piano in our living room for his students. Each week an assortment of them filed in and out of our house for their piano lessons. Lady was an astute student, too, and took a seat on top of the piano during the lessons. We soon learned she had a good ear, because cats can't read music, can they?

One blistering mid-July evening, we sat in lawn chairs on the back deck, sipping lemonade and fanning ourselves. The Delta breeze from the coast had finally begun to rustle the old walnut tree, announcing autumn's arrival and the promise of relief from the heat. The screen door was open and we heard the tinkle of piano keys. The music stopped and started again, this time with more bravado. We crept into the house, curious to see who the musician was. Lady strolled back and forth across the keys, playing her dissonant repertoire, and then stopped and took a bow, pointing her head toward her two outstretched paws.

Over time I learned Lady had eclectic tastes in the arts. I had studied fine art at SUNY Buffalo in New York and had finished up my degree in California. I especially enjoyed watercolor for its fluidity and immediacy. But the one drawback of painting in watercolor is that once the color meets paper, the marriage is forever. I put a great deal of planning and thought into my paintings before putting the brush to paper. Sometimes my paintings take several months to complete.

I had been working on a large painting with complicated patterns entitled *Seated Woman with Camellias*. The color palette for this painting was purples, reds and blues applied in delicate layers of glazes. The painting was to be hung in a few days time in a local gallery. I often kept my tools of the trade—brushes, palette, paints and water—set up on my drawing board to make it easier to get right to the task.

The painting was complete and I decided to go out for lunch to celebrate with a friend. When I returned, I again looked at my painting to see if there were any finishing touches that needed to be made before it was framed. To my horror someone *had* made some changes. My eyes followed a trail of small muddy paw prints that led from the drawing board onto the painting. The tracks, of pale mud, thankfully were erasable. But what of that purple blotch on the neck of the woman in my painting? My eyes went from the purple blotch and then back to Lady, who sat in her chair, fastidiously grooming her paws. She looked up at me with her beautiful amber eyes, which asked, "What's wrong? Don't you like the improvements I made?"

Psychic Cat

Kathryn Canan

A recent article in *Parade* magazine compared the intelligence of cats and dogs. According to the author, Kalee Thompson, "dogs are ahead by a nose" since they recognize more words and can be trained to do intricate tasks, serving as sheepherders, police dogs and service dogs. Okay, I'll concede that point. Anyone who tried to use a cat as a guide would end up at the top of a tree or burrowed under the covers of the nearest soft bed. I do take issue, however, with defining intelligence as the ability to be trained to do particular tasks. Our orange tabby, Chewbacca, takes the prize for ingenious, complex problem solving and weird psychic talents.

Unkind family members have described him as a "basketball with a Ping-Pong ball for a head." Certainly Chewie defies the purpose of his prescription-diet cat food: he seems to be missing the off switch that tells him to stop eating when he is full. We recently had to purchase a new raccoon- and squirrel-proof automatic cat feeder for use on short vacations because he had learned to open the old feeder; he would use one claw to delicately pull aside the trapdoor and let the food out whenever he wanted. He had also developed Fonzie moves to set off the feeder—a good whop of the paw in just the right place would send a shower of food down the chute. This new feeder was developed by a man with a similarly ingenious cat. My husband and I are taking bets on how soon Chewie will be able to hack into it.

A helpful cat, our Chewie. When he began marking the carpet in several places near the south wall of our house, we thought he was showing his age or reacting to cats and squirrels running along the top of the fence outside. But no. Turns out we had severe dry rot on that side of the house, and if we had listened to Chewie sooner, we would not have had to buy my husband a whole new wall for his birthday last year. I appreciate Chewie's taste in interior decorating, too; the new oak flooring is a huge improvement over the dingy gray carpet.

Chewie's psychic abilities showed up early in his life. It's true that cats don't fetch the way dogs do, but our cat does have an uncanny ability to find lost objects. I play early music on recorders and early flutes, and although Chewie rudely escapes under the bed at the sight of my soprano recorder, he still tries to participate. Before a performance one year at a local Renaissance fair, I rushed around the house, madly looking for a piece of music I wanted to play that day. It was nowhere to be found. Finally my husband noticed that Chewie was sitting on top of a tall file cabinet, on which he had never jumped before. Slowly swinging his tail to get our attention, he was carefully guarding the very piece of music I was seeking: "A Catch on the Midnight Cats."

Even better than detecting dry rot or locating missing music, Chewie is able to read my emotional wrangling and provide succinct answers to my dilemmas. There was one night in particular when during dinner —nothing Chewie does is unrelated to food— he solved a particularly thorny problem for me.

Growing up, I played the modern flute and piccolo, but in my early thirties I discovered the vast and gorgeous early music repertoire for the recorder and early wooden flutes. I soon joined the local chapter of the American Recorder Society to meet others infected by this bug. I learned about repertoire and style from those who had immersed themselves in Renaissance and baroque music for many years. One woman in particular took me on as her project. She came to my house when my youngest child, Robin, was just a few months old, and we formed an ensemble called Robin's Nest, which rehearsed while Robin napped nearby.

Soon others joined us, and the members of this ensemble nurtured my new enthusiasm and became my closest musical friends. In many ways, a musical ensemble resembles a marriage. Several musicians may "date" each other in informal playing sessions, assessing both personal and musical compatibility. Once a group gels into a regular ensemble, members make a commitment to show up, practice and always give their best. The friendships that form can be intense, since the object of all our work is to create beauty. Leaving an ensemble, then, can feel like a divorce.

Eventually the time came when I was no longer musically satisfied playing with the members of Robin's Nest. We seemed unable to solve problems with intonation, rhythm and ensemble skills, and our repertoire was limited to a narrow period of Renaissance music. I wanted to explore other genres of recorder music— medieval, baroque and contemporary—and I was ready to play at a more professional level. I had already begun to play with other musicians who challenged me in new ways.

It was an agonizing decision. Could I really leave these talented people who meant so much to me? I talked to other musicians about it. I talked to my husband, to my son who is also a musician. I talked to the air, talked in my sleep and I talked to the cat. Everyone listened politely but in the end reminded me that it was my decision alone. The image that kept coming up was of a bird ready to spread its wings and leave the nest. Certainly Robin's Nest had nurtured me for several years, and I was profoundly grateful for that. Month after month I put off the decision, coming home from rehearsals tired and frustrated.

At last one night my husband and I sat at the table, dinner over and the dishes before us. Once again I brought up the topic and said sadly, "I am so ready to leave the nest, the Robin's Nest." My husband sighed, dreading another evening of worrying over the same old topic, to go or stay. He was tired of the discussion. And apparently so was Chewie. In a sudden rush of loud movement he came through the cat door, jumped up on the table and deposited a dead bird on my now empty plate. Placing one paw on the dead bird, he sat up and looked proudly at me. "The bird has left the nest," I choked out when I had stopped laughing uncontrollably. My decision was made.

And it wasn't so bad, after all. My ensemble imported a new member who also played harpsichord. They added baroque music to their repertoire and two members took up the viola da gamba. My departure let them grow in new ways, and our friendships have stayed strong. Recently I have found myself remembering that episode, because I am now facing an empty nest of my own. Robin has just left for college, and Chewie's blunt nesting advice is useful once more.

My husband and I saw all the signs of a teenager ready to leave home during her senior year of high school. Senioritis hit hard, and we sympathized with her tirades over "stupid English poetry packets." She observed curfews but came home not a second too early. Family meals gave way to quick bites grabbed at fast-food restaurants or her own creative pasta concoctions. Somehow I found myself asking permission to use my own car, since her schedule was so full with swim team, film projects and an intricate social life. The college decision was really quite easy; Robin gave serious consideration only to colleges more than three hundred miles away. She wouldn't be popping home on weekends.

Chewie took to sleeping on Robin's bed.

My cousin once told me that when your kids are ready to leave home, you're ready to let them go. I repeated that mantra to everyone who asked me how I felt, hoping I would manage to believe it. When the day came at last, we drove nine hours to her new home and, feeling a bit like rats in a maze, navigated the tightly scheduled move-in procedure. We finished hauling her stuff upstairs to her dorm room, helped her make up her new bed and met her roommate. Suddenly the awkward moment arrived.

"So," she asked, "how long do you want to hang around?"

Chewie and the bird flashed into my mind. "I think we're ready to go." And we were.

Chewie is fourteen years old now, limping slightly from arthritis, and I doubt if he can ever again catch a bird or jump up on the table. But I look forward to his sage advice again, should I ever need it.

Maggie

Jerry and Donna White

My wife looked up from the newspaper she'd been reading. "You have to go get this dog."

A dog? We hadn't had a dog in years; our beloved Petunia and Whippet had spoiled us from any possible replacements.

She held the paper out toward me. "Read it. The dog is deaf. No one wants her." I knew by the tone in her voice, we were about to get a new dog.

"But what will I do with a deaf dog?" I asked.

"Train it," my wife replied.

"How can I train a deaf dog?" I pleaded.

"Teach it sign language," she said.

After years of marriage, I knew when I'd been overruled, and the very next day I went to the local pound.

Maggie was a cutie, a half-sized Dalmatian mix with a bobbed tail of all black. Maggie was only a couple months old. It was love at first sight. Attached as I had been to our old black labs, there was something about this little one I could not resist.

From the get-go Maggie was always super-alert to her surroundings. Unable to hear what was going on around her, she had to continually turn her head to be aware of events. When I took Maggie to the fields behind our house for our daily walk, I noticed she would keep a close watch on me. Even when she chased rabbits, she would periodically stop to check on my whereabouts.

As my wife predicted, I taught Maggie sign language. She learned three signals: "Come here," "Stop doing that" and "Look or go over there." We had had two dogs before, and they were all much smarter than me. Maggie was the smartest. She quickly learned to obey my hand signals, but she also realized that she did not have to obey the signals if she did not see them. Maggie developed the habit of not looking directly at me when she had a different idea of what she wanted to do next. She would face slightly to the left or right and could see me only from the corner of her eye. As soon as I gave a hand signal that Maggie did not agree with, she would turn a blind eye and proceed to do as she pleased, even if it meant on several occasions that a deaf dog was crossing a road. Maggie was lucky, as well as smart.

Friendly by nature and always sure of an enthusiastic welcome, Maggie liked to go visiting in the neighborhood. Of course, we had a dog-proof fence, but why should that have slowed her down? There were places to go and people to see.

The sight of someone calling out to his or her dog at the end of a day in an effort to bring it home is a common one—calling the dog's name hopefully at first, then impatiently for a few more minutes, and finally shouting the dog's name in anger before stomping back into the house with a muttered, "Your dog is gone again." But what do you do when the dog is deaf? You make it a point to learn all her visiting spots and check each one when it appears that she has once again climbed a tree.

Maggie's favorite place to visit was the neighborhood Waldorf School on the Unitarian Church grounds. She quickly became a favorite of the children, who called her by name amid a lot of petting. Of course, one of the teachers had to bring Maggie home.

"The children really like Maggie and they always look to see if she is waiting for them at recess," the young teacher said. "She is so cute and friendly. The children want to bring her into the classroom but we cannot allow that."

Maggie visited the school and church grounds many times before we discovered her tree-climbing trick. If Maggie went visiting and school was not in session, she would explore the church. More than once the church administrative assistant called me to inform me that Maggie was there. "Hello, Jerry? Well...Maggie is attending church again." She'd climb on a front-row bench and appear to show great interest in the proceedings. Nobody seemed to mind, but nobody was sure which set of religious beliefs she was observing. She liked all the groups but seemed especially fond of the Buddhist services. Everyone in that group knew her by name.

Since she was a puppy, she'd slept beside our bed, on my side. I still wake at night and reach down to make sure she is covered by her blanket, only to remember she is sleeping in our flower garden. We had to put her down at age twelve. Maggie has been in the garden for over three years now. We miss her every day.

Roxanne

Gordon M. Labuhn

It looked like a small, fuzzy black rock in the center of a busy four-lane street. Out of curiosity, I scooped it up as Karen and I zigzagged between cars on our way to get a steaming cup of coffee at our favorite greasy-spoon café. The fuzz ball was wet, soft, and it wiggled. The newborn's eyes were still matted shut.

"It's a kitten!"

In our café booth, we sipped our brew and Karen dipped her napkin into a glass of water to administer a therapeutic bath. Other customers gathered around our booth to see what we'd found and to share in the rescue. For a bassinet, the waitress loaned us a large coffee cup lined with a napkin. The kitten was so tiny that her head didn't even clear the rim. We named our newborn Rocky before we realized its gender; then we renamed her Roxanne.

Like every newborn, Roxanne required and received considerable TLC. We set up a nursery in the bathroom and embarked on a journey to save her. No matter what we tried, we couldn't get her to take nourishment. With an eyedropper, we thought we succeeded in getting one or two drops of warm milk into Roxanne's mouth, but we weren't sure.

In desperation, we rushed to the local veterinarian's office. Gently the vet examined our tiny friend and we were given ointment for her infected eyes. "You should know this now," the vet said gently. "She isn't likely to survive." Instantly, Karen and I became undaunted, determined to win her battle for life. Roxanne had no one but us to care for her.

Karen, a registered nurse, took her ten days of accrued vacation time to work a miracle. Our six-year-old neighbor, Julie, volunteered to be an assistant nursemaid. Young girls are a great help to newborn kittens during the day, but nights were a struggle.

Our rescue Roxanne's routine went like this: every forty-five minutes, day and night, the eyedropper wet kitty's lips with warm milk, and four times a day the ointment was applied to her eyes. After two days Roxanne's eyes were getting better. Ours, on the other hand, were getting redder. Sleep deprivation chipped away at our stamina.

Progress in feeding was slow, but with persistence

nourishment dribbled into our infant drop by drop. On day four Roxanne tried to walk. Wobbly and unsure, she promptly fell into a saucer of milk. It was drink or drown. She quickly weaned herself off the eyedropper. We cried.

Like every parent of a newborn, we worried about what the future would hold. Young Julie had fallen in love with Roxanne and was desperate to keep her, but pets weren't allowed in her family's complex. Both Karen and I traveled for business frequently; we couldn't take care of her long term. Once Roxanne was over her initial survival crisis, we planned to seek a permanent home for her.

Karen taught Julie how to knit, and together they made a one-inch-wide, five-inch-long soft strip, which I dubbed a bookmark. When Roxanne was not sleeping on the bookmark, she played with it vigorously. She was becoming a wide-eyed scamp, always on the move. Her prognosis for life turned from gloomy to hopeful.

The twists and turns in a kitten's life are not much different than for any vulnerable newborn. I was scheduled as a guest speaker at a meeting in a Springfield, Illinois, hospital. Roxanne couldn't be left alone, of course, so at the age of three weeks she had her first long-distance car trip in a towel-lined cardboard box. She was accompanied by a saucer, a baby bottle of milk, a dab of soft kitten food and her woven bookmark.

Karen came along on the trip and planned to wait for me in the car and read while Roxanne slept.

On my way to the meeting room in the hospital I passed a nursing station. One nurse was crying softly as her coworkers gathered around her.

"Anything I can do to help?" I asked.

A nurse at the edge of the small group shook her head sadly, still looking at her friend, while she whispered to me, "Oh, it's so sad. This morning she accidently ran over her daughter's kitten."

Ah, I could help, after all. I whispered in return, "Don't let her leave. I'll be right back."

Believe me, there is no greater pleasure in this world than to give a gift of love to a wounded soul. Karen and I brought in Roxanne with her box, saucer, bottle of milk and yarn bookmark. Willeen, the crying nurse, adopted Roxanne quicker than a cat could blink. She left work with the goal of taking her daughter out of school for the day to have a healing celebration. We had found a permanent home for Roxanne where the bonds of affection would be strong.

Story's end? Not quite!

A year later it was my good fortune to be scheduled for a return visit to Springfield. On our trip Karen and I reminisced about our experience in saving Roxanne. Was she still alive? Did she have any major health problems? Would we get a chance to see her? When we arrived at the hospital, our questions were answered by Willeen, who was waiting for us at the door.

"Roxanne is fine. Would you like to see her?"

"Yes, we would love to," we said in unison. A quick trip to Willeen's home during the lunch hour was arranged.

It was a thrill for Karen and me to see Roxanne comfortably lounging in an old apple tree. She was so black and silky, so at peace with her life. *Amazement* is a weak word to describe our shock in discovering the tattered and faded yarn bookmark draped over Roxanne's perch. We coaxed her to come down. Roxanne picked up her bookmark, came down the tree bottom first, made a beeline to her cat door and disappeared into the safety of her home.

"I can't believe it," I said. "She still has the bookmark that Julie made, after all this time."

"Yes," Willeen said. "She carries it everyplace she goes. Last year I washed it, and she sat on top of the washing machine and meowed the whole time it was being washed. I felt so sorry for her that I gave it back to her without putting it in the dryer."

Roxanne still holds a place in our hearts. I like to think that Karen and I, like the bookmark we gave her, hold a small place in hers, too.

High Energy

Mark Lukas

It's a crisp, sunny Sunday afternoon in Central Florida as Zak heads down the driveway and turns his truck onto the street, towing his new Jet Ski and trailer behind him. A placid golf course community with dogwood-lined streets, our new neighborhood is perfect for a family of four. *We'll all be happy here,* I think, still standing in the garage with tools in my hand, as Zak turns and waves to me. This is the last time I'll see my sixteen-year-old son alive.

Just minutes before we'd had a father-son chuckle together as Zak searched for bolts to install the new license plate on the trailer. Listening to his fingers riffle through the metal in the nuts-and-bolts storage bin, I asked him what he was looking for. "I need bigger nuts," he answered back casually. Immediately he froze when he registered what he'd said to his dad. He turned and looked over at me with a sly smile. He knew what a mistake that comment was.

Sixteen-year-old boys have very little fear; they all think they're invincible. Zak and his friend from the high school soccer team, Jason Lewis, died that night when the Jet Ski sucked up a line from a crab trap, disabling the engine. They'd set out into the Gulf of Mexico at about 2:00 p.m., and when Zak didn't show up for dinner with our friends that night, we tried not to worry. A cold front blew in from the North, and the Coast Guard would not search over the water because of the fog. A fishing boat found the boys nine miles out the next morning. They hadn't made it through the night, dying of hypothermia.

Zak's death was the beginning of the end of my life as I knew it. My twenty-year marriage dissolved; my relationship with my daughter faltered. I lost my whole family the day Zak died.

Zak was my hero. His life was full. He lived to play. He was very popular and he loved people. I think his goal in life was to make people laugh. His popularity came from being a great athlete; he was always one of the first picked and everyone wanted to be on Zak's team. True, Zak was not a good loser, but he was often a winner. By the time he was twelve, he was dribbling a soccer ball past me and his soccer coach, laughing as he zipped by. He played soccer at a high level on a traveling competitive team, and he played varsity soccer as a high school freshman.

Zak didn't like working out alone with a soccer ball. At a professional soccer game we'd gone to watch as a family, he thought he spotted the answer to this dilemma: during the opening ceremony an amazing border collie dribbled a soccer ball with incredible speed and skill. We met up with the owner after the game.

Zak reached down to pet the border collie and asked, "What's the dog's name?"

"Silk," the proud owner told us.

That was it. We were hooked on the idea of having a soccer dog like Silk in our family.

"Zak, if you had a dog like Silk, would you put down the video games and go outside for soccer every day?" I asked him.

He smiled and nodded.

We purchased an Australian shepherd with the intent of teaching her how to play soccer. Did it really happen? No. With our busy lives, no one put the time into the training. Instead of being a soccer dog, Kobe ended up being really good with a Frisbee.

Soon after Zak's death I found myself living alone. It was time to try and teach a dog how to play soccer. It was, I thought, a way in which I could feel somehow close to Zak. I derived some small comfort in following through on something we'd talked about doing together.

When I went to pick out a border collie pup, there were two males roughing each other up and a scrawny little female who just sat there and watched her brothers fight. I pointed at the female. "I'll take that one." I named her Ms. Z after Zak. At first she was an awful lot like Zak—feisty and high maintenance, full of energy and very demanding. How could I channel this into soccer playing?

Turned out that I owned the perfect training ground—a fourplex housing unit. One of the units needed a new floor put in, and to save money, I was doing the work myself, down on my hands and knees every day, putting in new tile. The puppy would go with me every day and roam around the apartment while I tried to get things done. Of course, she wanted to play. To keep her occupied, I had a hard rubber ball that was really too big for Ms. Z to get her mouth around. I tossed the ball and she chased it. A simple game.

She would whine and talk to the ball, venting her frustration and inability to get her mouth around it. Once she maneuvered the ball back to me, I stopped whatever I was doing and I heaped big praise on her and then threw the ball again. After a couple days of this and no small amount of doggy swearing and frustration, she finally learned how to maneuver the ball to me. One day something seemed to click in her mind: she realized that she had to bring me that ball if she wanted me to play with her.

Anyone who has ever spent time with a border collie knows that they need a job. Bred to herd, if they don't have something to do, if they don't have several hours of exercise a day, it won't be pretty. Sooner or later they will eat your house. Soccer became Ms. Z's job. She was getting pretty good at it, too. After a few weeks of playing soccer every day, we went to visit my sister and her twin eight-year-old girls. One of the girls tossed the ball to Ms. Z and she caught it! I still remember their excitement and astonishment.

Catching a soccer ball between her wide open mouth and her paws has become Ms. Z's signature statement. As time went on, Ms. Z really started to think all humans were born to play soccer with her and she would adore anyone who would touch a soccer ball. She would play with anyone. It didn't matter where you were or what you were wearing. If you touched the ball, then you became her instant best friend.

I started to wonder just how far this could go. I went out and purchased two female border collie pups and named them Sweeper and Keeper, and did they ever live up to their names. Then I found Bek—yes, he is named after David Beckham—in a litter of brown-and-white border collie puppies. My intention was to become a soccer dog breeder and trainer. With three females and one male, this would be the start of something big. Soccer Collies was formed.

Soccer Collies is much different today than when we started. The business has evolved from a one-on-one encounter with a soccer dog to a group activity. Here's a description of what we do: groups of kids ages two to ninety-two play the goalkeeper position as an incredibly talented soccer dog scores goals. A lot of goals! It's a competition involving speed and agility, as the dogs quickly show their human competitors who has faster feet. There's always laughter, especially when adults play against the dogs.

In the past years Soccer Collies have worked everywhere—from companies like Google and Purina to sports organizations like Major League Soccer and Women's Professional Soccer. My dogs have entertained the crowd at places like the U.S. Open, Nokia Plaza and the Staples Center.

Training soccer dogs and promoting the soccer dog movement have become my life's purpose. Nothing will ever replace my son, Zak, but working with the dogs gave me a reason to live again.

ABOUT THE CONTRIBUTORS

Elaine Ambrose

Elaine Ambrose is the co-author of *Menopause Sucks* and *Drinking with Dead Women Writers*. Her short stories and feature articles appear in several anthologies and magazines, and she owns Mill Park Publishing. She organizes "Write by the River" writers' retreats in Idaho and creates a sassy blog called "Midlife Cabernet." Find more details at www.ElaineAmbrose.com.

Hal Bernton

Hal Bernton is a journalist who works for *The Seattle Times*. He lives in Portland, Oregon with his wife, Ann, and their basset hound, Maverick.

Sheryl J. Bize Boutte

Sheryl J. Bize Boutte is a Northern California writer and management consultant. More of her short stories, poetry and commentary can be seen at www.sjbb-talkinginclass.blogspot.com/.

Robyn Boyer

Robyn Boyer's daytime job is to write about public policy, politics and people. This is the first story she has written about animals. She lives in Sacramento, California, and has a daughter and a cat.

Maryellen Burns

Maryellen Burns has been involved in the word trade for more than forty years, working with writers, publishers, libraries and booksellers in editing, research, public relations and events planning. Her work has appeared in newspapers, literary anthologies, *Smithsonian* and *Cooking Light*. When not writing, she's engaged in helping others get their words on the page and into the marketplace. Visit her at booktalksacramento.blogspot.com.

Kathryn Canan

Whenever the family cabin in Montana is buried in snow, Kathryn Canan lives in California with her husband and two psychotic cats. She is a freelance writer, Latin tutor, and early music teacher and performer; she has recorded CDs of medieval and Renaissance music with Briddes Roune and the New Queen's Ha'penny Consort. Her master's thesis on Anglo-Saxon medicine has made her one of the few experts in diseases caused by malevolent elves.

Louise Crawford

Louise (AKA L.F.) Crawford writes under both names depending on the genre. In her next Blalize/Zoloski mystery, *Blaize of Trouble,* Blaize rescues a bulldog after his owner is murdered, wrestles her bra from his slobbery mouth, solves a kidnapping and plans her wedding, all in the same week! For darker suspense/thriller Dexter fans, check out *Born in Blood,* and for more information visit Crawford's websites: www.lfcrawford.com and www.louisecrawfordbooks.com.

Tish Davidson

Tish Davidson writes and lives with dogs in Fremont, California. Her nonfiction has been published by Scholastic, Adams Media, and many magazines and newspapers. Currently she is writing a mystery novel whose main character is a professional pet sitter. Davidson can be contacted at tish_davidson@yahoo.com.

Trina Drotar

Trina Drotar (poet, writer, visual artist) has been widely published and is currently working on *In the Night Garden,* a collection of poetry, prose and art. Cats in need always find her. Reach her at TrinaLDrotar@gmail.com.

E. G. Fabricant

E. G. Fabricant writes and lives in Sacramento, California. His first short story collection, *Matters Familiar,* is available in e-book format from Barnes & Noble, iTunes, Smashwords and Sony. Connect to E. G.'s blog and sample stories online at egfabricant.com and follow him as egfabricant on Facebook and Twitter. His email is egf@egfabricant.com; if you prefer pulp over electrons, write to him at P. O. Box 19170, Sacramento, CA 95819-0170.

Chris Fowler

Chris Fowler is a born and bred California girl who divides her time between her devotion to family, the fire department and roller derby. She is an aspiring non-fiction writer. This is her first publication.

Pam Giarrizzo

Pam Giarrizzo is a retired attorney living in Northern California with her husband Phil, a political consultant. Their son, Zack, is a freshman in college. Pam is a founding member of the Sacramento Women's Action Network (SWAN), a giving circle that provides funding to nonprofit organizations serving the Sacramento area. She also serves on the boards of the California Museum for History, Women and the Arts, and the Camellia Network, which assists young people who are transitioning from foster care to adulthood. She is the author of the

Sacramento Vegan blog, which identifies restaurants in the Sacramento area offering menu choices for vegans.

Ed Goldman

Ed Goldman is a daily business columnist, the author of 4,000 newspaper and magazine features, three books and the musical *Friday@5*. His new comedy, *Jews Don't Kayak,* will be produced in early 2013. Contact him at goldman4@ earthlink.net.

Meera Klein

Meera Ekkanath Klein is a writer who lives in Davis, CA with her family. She is currently working on a story about her coon hound, Duke, the original dog of leisure.

Dena Kouremetis

Consumer journalist, author and would-be shrink, Dena Kouremetis loves to examine life from a midlife perspective. She is a national columnist for three channels at Examiner.com, has authored, co-authored and contributed content to dozens of books, and loves to speak to groups about how our online presence says volumes about us. She welcomes visits to her website at communic8or.com.

Charles Kuhn

Charles Kuhn is an accomplished writer in the areas of mystery, non-fiction and adventure. He has published short stories in various magazines, self-published and writes for local writers groups, including the poetry group for the local Sacramento Multiple Sclerosis Association. Mr. Kuhn and his wife reside in Citrus Heights, CA.

Gordon M. Labuhn

Gordon M. Labuhn is the author of *Murder Has Two Faces* (2011), a feature article journalist for a Detroit newspaper, the screen writer and movie producer of one nationally promoted movie, a winner of the National PR.PI award, and has won first place in the Bayview writers essay competitions in 2008.

Mark Lukas

Mark Lukas, a Soccer Dog Guru, travels nationally with his famous Soccer Collies. The world's greatest soccer dogs, Ms. Z and BEK, rescued Lukas from old age. Now they bring back child-like behavior to everyone who has forgotten how to be a kid. Not to mention the Soccer Collies help train and adopt soccer dogs as they promote youth soccer and dog rescue. SoccerCollies@gmail.com.

Jennifer O'Neill-Pickering

Jennifer O'Neill-Pickering is a writer and an artist living in Sacramento, California. Her writing is featured in many publications including *Sacramento Anthology: 100 Poems, Earth's Daughters, Sacramento News and Review* and *Medusa's Kitchen.* Her poem, "I Am the Creek," is included in the Sacramento site-specific sculpture, Open Circle. She's published two books: *Poems with the Element of Water and Mandala Art, Poetry, and Instruction.* Contact her at her blog, Jennifer's Art and Words or at jenniferartist@att.net.

Sue Pearson

Sue Pearson has been a journalist for more than 30 years. Writing is her passion and animals fuel her soul. She has staked out a little piece of heaven on 6 acres in the Northern California foothills where her four horses, two dogs and a cat inspire her every day.

Morton Rumberg

Mort Rumberg was a volunteer at the Animal Welfare League of Alexandria, Virginia, for eight years, where the story of Hammer was told to him by the director of animal welfare. He has written several novels, one of which has won a national award, and many short stories that have won awards in national competitions. He now resides in Gold River, California, with his American Eskimo dogs, Yuki and Kori. Visit his website at mmrumberg.com.

Finley Taylor

Finley Taylor lives, works and writes in Northern California. She and her husband are thrilled to be expecting twin girls in summer 2012, but Finley will always consider Bridgette her first "kid."

Suzanne Tomlinson

Suzanne Tomlinson lives on a ranch tending her beloved horses. She has learned how to be her own best friend and is grateful for the journey that has led her to inner peace.

Katherine Traci

Kate (or Katherine) Traci is a beach girl at heart who now lives in Surprise Arizona with two cats, including the heroic Simon, and one dog, who might be her furry soul mate. She patiently waits for her next adventure on a dark starry night in the Arizona desert.

Jerry and Donna White

Jerry White had a career in the military and in real estate. He now teaches in the Earth Science department of a local community college. Donna White is a retired nurse who now spends her time in the garden. She is known as the "compost lady" of the neighborhood.

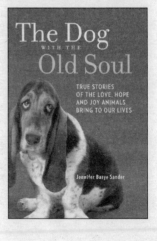

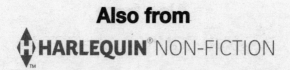